CW00740512

BE

Auckland

Simone Egger

Colour-Coding & Maps

Each chapter has a colour code along the banner at the top of the page which is also used for text and symbols on maps (eg all venues reviewed in the Highlights chapter are orange on the maps). The fold-out maps inside the front and back covers are numbered from 1 to 8. All sights and venues in the text have map references; eg, (5, C1) means Map 5, grid reference C1. See p64 for map symbols.

Prices

Multiple prices listed with reviews (eg [\$10/5]) usually indicate adult/concession admission to a venue. Concession prices can include senior, student, member or coupon discounts. Meal cost and room rate categories are listed at the start of the Eating and Sleeping chapters, respectively.

Text Symbols

☎ telephone

✉ address

▣ email/website address

$ admission

☽ opening hours

ⓘ information

🚍 bus

🚆 train

⚓ ferry

Ⓟ parking available

✕ on site/nearby eatery

🧒 child-friendly venue

Best of Auckland
1st edition – October 2006

Published by Lonely Planet Publications Pty Ltd
ABN 36 005 607 983

Australia Head Office, Locked Bag 1, Footscray, Vic 3011
☎ 03 8379 8000, fax 03 8379 8111
▣ talk2us@lonelyplanet.com.au
USA 150 Linden St, Oakland, CA 94607
☎ 510 893 8555, toll free 800 275 8555
fax 510 893 8572
▣ info@lonelyplanet.com
UK 72–82 Rosebery Ave, Clerkenwell, London
EC1R 4RW
☎ 020 7841 9000, fax 020 7841 9001
▣ go@lonelyplanet.co.uk

This title was commissioned in Lonely Planet's Melbourne office and produced by: **Commissioning Editors** Jessa Boanas-Dewes, Errol Hunt **Coordinating Editors** Charlotte Orr, Martine Lleonart **Coordinating Cartographer** Diana Duggan **Layout Designer** Pablo Gastar **Managing Cartographer** Corinne Waddell **Cover Designer** Rebecca Dandens **Project Manager** Rachel Imeson **Thanks to** David Connolly, Helen Christinis, Sally Darmody, Annie Dundas, James Ellis, Jennifer Garrett, Jane Healy, Katie Lynch, Michael Lynden-Bell, Kate McDonald, Nick Potter, Chantelle Rae, Fiona Siseman, Simon Tillema, Jonny Wartmann, Celia Wood.

Photographs by Simone Egger except for the following: p6 Rob Suisted/Tourism New Zealand; p7, p43 Gareth Eyres/Tourism New Zealand; p8, p10, p17, p20, p25, p30, p39, p49, p50 Tourism Auckland; p12 Pest5 @ Disrupt Gallery; p14 Auckland Zoo; p14 Tourism New Zealand; p18 Anders Blomqvist/Lonely Planet Images; p23, p30, p31 Kieran Scott/Tourism New Zealand; p24 Scott Venning/Tourism New Zealand; p27, p37, p38 David Wall/Lonely Planet Images; p35 Peter Bennetts/Lonely Planet Images; p45 Hilton Hotel. **Cover photograph** Sky jumper, Sky Tower, Auckland, Peter Bennetts/Lonely Planet Images. All images are copyright of the photographers unless otherwise indicated. Many of the images in this guide are available for licensing from Lonely Planet Images: www.lonelyplanetimages.com.

ISBN 1 74104 759 5

Printed through Colorcraft Ltd, Hong Kong.
Printed in China

Contents

From the Publisher

AUTHOR & PHOTOGRAPHER
Simone Egger

Simone lives in Melbourne and works as a freelance writer and photographer. She writes for a range of online and print publications, works regularly with the Asylum Seekers Resource Centre, writes for children and for Lonely Planet.

Travel has always been in her bio, with much time spent slung with a camera in overseas cities. Aucklanders, volcanoes and black-sand beaches keep drawing Simone back to New Zealand, with which she's smitten.

Simone maintains an art practice in photography. Her commercial commissions include theatre work, editorial travel and product shots.

Thanks to the following Aucklanders for their input and generosity: Brett Atkinson, Melissa and Bianca, Jane Healy, Pip McLeod, James Thomas and Jeremy Hubbard. At Lonely Planet, thanks to Errol and Jessa. And at home, thanks Kingi.

LONELY PLANET AUTHORS
Why is our travel information the best in the world? It's simple: our authors are independent, dedicated travellers. They don't research using just the Internet or phone, and they don't take freebies in exchange for positive coverage. They travel widely, to all the popular spots and off the beaten track. They personally visit thousands of hotels, restaurants, cafés, bars, galleries, palaces, museums and more – and they take pride in getting all the details right, and telling it how it is. For more, see the authors section on **www.lonelyplanet.com**.

SEND US YOUR FEEDBACK
We love to hear from travellers – your comments keep us on our toes and help make our books better. Our well-travelled team reads every word on what you loved or loathed about this book. Although we cannot reply individually to postal submissions, we always guarantee that your feedback goes straight to the appropriate authors, in time for the next edition – and the most useful submissions are rewarded with a free book. To send us your updates – and find out about Lonely Planet events, newsletters and travel news – visit our award-winning website: **www.lonelyplanet.com/feedback**.

Note: We may edit, reproduce and incorporate your comments in Lonely Planet products such as guidebooks, websites and digital products, so let us know if you don't want your comments reproduced or your name acknowledged. For a copy of our privacy policy visit **www.lonelyplanet.com/privacy**.

Introducing Auckland

Auckland (Tamaki Makaurau in Maori) is a stunning city. The hum of its hefty commercial heart is modulated by the expanse of its island-studded harbour and by grassy parklands that blanket its dozens of sleeping volcanoes.

Downtown: brisk phone calls and keyboard workouts in the city's many office towers control the region's economy. And its container ports and airport shift the bulk of the country's goods. Auckland has evolved as the centre of New Zealand's media, design and fashion industries, and is home to a third of its population. It behaves as though it doesn't know it's no longer the country's capital.

Auckland is a youngster at just 165 years. Experiencing a massive growth spurt in the past 20 years, it continues to develop at a rate of knots. Its full cultural and sporting calendar continues to expand. And its population is expected to double within a decade; a population that is among the city's greatest assets. Its people are what make Auckland unique: from the rest of NZ and from anywhere in the world.

Aucklanders identify with around 30 different cultures; largely represented by Maori, Pacific Islander, European (Pakeha) and Asian. The mix results in a city characterised by general exuberance, with a respect for nature, and underpinned with mythology and meaning. (Not to mention an outrageously good variety of food.) It's a friendly city: human in scale, and humbled by nature.

A spaceage presence on Auckland's skyline: Sky Tower (p10)

Neighbourhoods

Sprawling Auckland is a narrow strip of land sandwiched between two picturesque harbours: Manukau in the south and Waitemata in the north.

The commercial action clings to Waitemata Harbour, with office blocks watching over sailboats that flit around islands like moths around a light. The city's **Viaduct Harbour** and **Princes Wharf** are hubs for harbour tours and dining options. Visible from the waterfront is the quaint waterside suburb of **Devonport**, which juts out of the North Shore.

On the ferry outta town

Ferries dock and depart from the Ferry Building, adjacent to the Britomart Transport Centre, from where buses and trains network out across Auckland.

Shoppers trawl along the parallel Queen and High Sts for tissue-wrapped designs or mass-made bargains. Queen St runs south, within a few blocks of the ever-present Sky Tower, and past big-venue-studded Mayoral Dr to Newton's K Rd. The city's most interesting shops and cafés are on **K Road**. Tame by day, the energy ramps up after dark when revellers spill from its clubs and bars.

The demure **Ponsonby** lies west of K Rd. Ponsonby Rd (www.ponsonbyroad.co.nz) stretches north for around a kilometre, crammed with designer cafés, boutiques, book shops and galleries. Its restaurants and bars attract a polished, polite crowd. Ponsonby makes a fine alternative to staying downtown.

Further west is Auckland's next-big-thing suburb, **Kingsland**. New North Rd has plentiful stellar cafés and stores clustered in a tiny stretch.

Hugging the city's magnificent green Domain in the city's east is **Parnell** (www.parnell.net.nz). It's like a grown-up Ponsonby: its quaint Victoriana villages attracting a more mature crowd. It is home to a number of revered eateries, a pod of commercial galleries and boutiques.

It's all punctuated with volcanic cones, within a 30-minute walk of Downtown, and well connected by the city's transport network. Travel out a little further to experience some of the region's glorious geography.

Within an hour southwest of the CBD are the fern-filled folds of the **Waitakere Ranges**. Its bushwalks through lush forest rival its thundering black-sand beaches for breathtaking beauty.

The **islands of the Hauraki Gulf** (just outside Waitemata Harbour) make great days away from the city. Explore lava caves and hike to the summit of Rangitoto, or while away an afternoon in a vineyard on Waiheke.

Itineraries

If you've only got a day or three in Auckland, the following itineraries cover most of the city's sights. Each takes a day, so could be strung together for a diverse diet of sights. Also consider taking a day out; see Trips & Tours (p22).

WORST OF AUCKLAND
- The city's spaghetti of motorways
- Another 'Delayed' on the bus info sign
- Poor premium-priced coffee at big-ticket tourist sights

The Auckland Super Pass (adult/child $70/40) is good for families; it includes entry to Sky Tower, Kelly Tarlton's, Rainbow's End and a trip to Rangitoto. It's valid for four weeks and available from each sight.

TIME-POOR PERSON'S TOUR

It's possible to see all of Auckland in about five minutes; the views from Sky Tower stretch for 80km. Come back down to earth and pick up proof of your visit by buying a Kiwiana key ring along Queen St or a made-in-New Zealand masterpiece from one of High St's designer stores. Look in at the New Gallery, then huff up the Albert Park hill for a quick convene with nature. Lunch in Vulcan Lane, then make for the waterfront, zip over to Devonport, then back to the Viaduct to settle in for a sunset beverage.

SEE BEYOND THE CBD

Wake up in Ponsonby with a bowl of café latte before exercising your credit card in Ponsonby Rd's bookshops and boutiques. Then take a trip down trippy K Rd, stopping for a Samoan curry, kebab or noodle dish. Just over Grafton Bridge, give your afternoon to the museum's Maori and other memorable collections and its magnificent grounds, the Domain – built on the remains of a volcano and *pa* (fortified Maori village).

FRINGE DWELLERS

Breakfast and browse on New North Rd, and discover why Kingsland's the talk of the town. Then go west to a hat trick of purpose-built places on the edge of the city: the charmingly downbeat Museum of Transport and Technology (Motat), the Zoo (at 2pm when the coy kiwi comes out) and the bird-magnet lake in Western Springs Park.

View of north Auckland from high in the sky

Highlights

AUCKLAND MUSEUM/TAMAKI PAENGA HIRA (4, E5)

This monumental museum, set in the glorious Domain (p18), presents all aspects of life in Auckland through its vast collections, interactive displays, performances and re-creations.

Get inside the mind of a moa by experiencing the museum's natural history gallery, which runs the gamut on the region's physical world: from pre-Maori through European as it relates to the land and sea. There are over 1.5 million specimens: freeze-dried, pickled, stuffed and skewered. Plus plenty of live specimens like those under the glass boardwalk in the rock pool. Other theme galleries centre on people, with displays on social histories, ethnology and arts. Kid-friendly activities include opportunities to dress up, open drawers full of big hairy spiders and to hold mealworms (who's squirming more: the worm or them?). The War Memorial on the top floor is both a museum exploring New Zealand's history with war (from the 19th century to the peace-keeping assignments of today), as well as a site of commemoration.

The museum has occupied its imposing hill-top spot since 1929, and has grown to accommodate its ever-increasing collections.

The spiffy Grand Atrium, which should be open by the time you read this, will increase the museum's exhibition capacity by 60%. The museum shop sells Kiwiana, including music, jewellery and books, plus other bibs and bobs (like *tiki*, Maori greenstone neck ornaments, and *teko teko*, Maori carvings of full-figured humans, often in a defiant stance with tongue poking out).

INFORMATION

- ☎ 309 0443
- 🖥 www.aucklandmuseum.com
- ✉ off Domain Dr, Auckland Domain
- $ suggested donation adult/child $5/free
- 🕙 10am-5pm
- ℹ Manaia (☎ 306 7048; adult/child $15/12) is a performance of Maori song and dance that starts at 11am, noon and 1.30pm. Highlights Tours (☎ 306 7048; adult/child $10/5; 🕙 10.30am).
- 🚌 Link
- P $5 per hour
- ✗ café

VIADUCT HARBOUR (2, A1)

Founded on a propensity for nonmarking shoes, tycoons, superyachts (read large and luxurious) and a healthy sense of competition, Viaduct Harbour is the 'City of Sails' pin-up location.

Developed as the stage for NZ to defend its ownership of the sailing world's ultimate prize – the America's Cup (www.americascup.com) – the harbour (developed in the late '90s) is a glitzy, tourist-centric concentration of plazas, promenades, luxury apartments, bars and restaurants. And all overlooking that placid water that buoys so many gently bobbing boats. It's a fitting

INFORMATION

- 🖥 www.viaduct.co.nz
- ✉ Hobson Wharf, Quay St
- 🚌 Link
- ✂ Viaduct Harbour & Princes Wharf (p32)

DON'T MISS

- Burning about the bay in an America's Cup yacht, with Sail NZ (☎ 359 5987; www.sailnewzealand.co.nz; Viaduct Harbour; adult/child from $135/110)
- Swimming with sea mammals on a Dolphin & Whale Safari (☎ 357 6032; www.dolphinsafari.co.nz; Viaduct Harbour; adult/child $140/100; ☸ 10.30am-4pm)
- Whipping up the water in a fast inflatable with Ocean Rafting (☎ 577 3194; www.oceanrafting.co.nz; Viaduct Harbour; one-hour tour adult/child $70/35)

'Business dude' isn't allowed to skateboard

Come worship the big keel

address for the **Maritime Museum** (p17) and Maritime Trail, a paved walkway around the rim of the harbour's basin that's inlaid with brass information plaques highlighting key aspects of Auckland's symbiosis with the sea.

In addition to viewing this major transport hub, you can play sailor yourself by commandeering your own boat for a cruise around the harbour and signing up for a sailing lesson (see p17).

Summer sees an outdoor stage occupied by a range of performers singing, playing or acting. It's also the season for outdoor cinema (www.openair.co.nz), when classic and current films screen during February.

SKY TOWER (2, A3)

Million-dollar views with change from $20 – at 328m, Sky Tower is the pinnacle of the **Sky City** complex. It's a hedonistic hub, with 1600 flashing jingly machines and 100 gaming tables in its two casinos, plus cinemas, dining options and a five-star hotel.

Take the glass elevator (No 1) 186m up for 40 ear-popping seconds to the **Main Observation Level**. From here you can count around 20 of the city's 48 volcanoes (or count the number of vertigo sufferers). See for up to 80km: east to the Hauraki Gulf, north to Waitemata Harbour, south across the sprawling city and west to the Waitakere Ranges. For $3 more you can go 34m up to the second observation level, **Sky Deck**.

Vertigo Climb (☎ 368 1917; www .4vertigo.com; adult/child $145/75) has a two-hour tour with a 15-minute climb up through the interior mast to an external crow's-nest. Or, take the plunge from NZ's highest base-jumping platform (192m) with **Sky Jump** (☎ 368 1835; www.skyjump.co.nz; $195).

INFORMATION

- ☎ 363 6400
- 🖳 www.skycityauckland.co.nz
- ✉ cnr Federal & Victoria Sts
- 💲 adult/child/family $18/8/44
- 🕑 8.30am-10.30pm Sun-Thu, to 11.30pm Fri & Sat
- ℹ Auckland Visitor Information Centre (☎ 363 7182; www.aucklandnz .com; Sky Tower Atrium; 🕑 8am-8pm)
- 🚇 Link
- 🍴 Sky Lounge & Orbit (revolving restaurant)

AERIE AERIAL

The mast atop Sky Tower transmits a dizzying amount of information: from daytime soaps and talkback shows to mobile-phone conversations and weather measurements. And it's the world's single largest conduit of FM stations.

DEVONPORT (MAP 5)

The charismatic harbourside suburb of Devonport is a 10-minute ferry ride from central Auckland. Its beaches and proximity to, but physical separation from, the CBD has nurtured an unruffled holidayesque ambience.

Devonport was one of the earliest areas of European settlement, and many of its Victorian and Edwardian buildings have been preserved. It's little surprise, then, that the main street, Victoria Rd, proffers plenty of shops in which to mooch around antiques and books, plus galleries galore (including ceramics, glass and jewellery) and cafés.

Or, break out the bucket and spade at **Devonport Beach**, **Duders Beach** or **Cheltenham Beach**, with grassy picnic area and wharf from which to drop a line. Walkers are rewarded with cracking views over to the city throng from **Mt Victoria**

INFORMATION

- www.tourismnorthshore.org.nz
- ℹ North Shore iSite (☎ 446 0677; 3 Victoria Rd, Devonport; ⏲ 8.30am-5pm)
- ⚓ from Auckland Ferry Bldg: adult/child return $9/4.40
- ✗ Devonport (p35)

Trot past the toadstools on Mt Victoria

(Devonport's highest volcanic cone), laced with terraces and tunnels and a disappearing gun – a reminder of its fortified history. (Though the gun's single shot was fired not in anger, it did anger many residents whose windows shattered from the reverberation.)

Devonport still has a defence presence – the headquarters for the NZ Navy. Get the full story at the **Navy Museum** (☎ 445 5186; Spring St; admission by donation; ⏲ 10am-4.30pm). Learn about the area's industrial and social history at the **Devonport Museum** (☎ 445 2661; www.devonportmuseum.org .nz; 31a Vauxhall Rd; admission by donation; ⏲ 2-4pm Sat & Sun). Or get in quick for what may be the last chance to see the quirky collections in Jacksons Muzeum (☎ 446 0466; Victoria Rd; ⏲ 11am-4pm) – the 'muzeum' is for sale late 2006.

The iSite visitors centre can help you locate one of the area's abundance of B&Bs should you choose to make more than a day of it.

DON'T MISS

- **Depot Artspace** (☎ 963 2331; www.depotartspace.co.nz; 28 Clarence St; ⏲ 10am-5pm Mon-Sat), an excellent community-run gallery
- Legging it along a section of the North Shore Coastal Walk, part of Te Araroa (www.teararoa.org.nz) that, by 2008, will run the length of NZ
- The **Trash & Treasure Market** (Friendly Societies Hall; 93 Victoria St; ⏲ 10am-3pm 1st Sun of every month)
- Spotting the houses and regular haunts of the area's many literary giants – including Janet Frame and Maurice Duggan – mapped on the self-guided North Shore Literary Walks brochure available from the visitors centre

K ROAD (MAP 7)

Anything goes on K Rd – the city's boho heartland. Lads lounge on outdoor furniture puffing on hookahs. Saloon-style doors swing open to reveal sex toys and costumes. Maori-inspired couture graces a shop window. Chic black-clad people group around giant artworks holding champagne flutes aloft. A barrage of signs sell Chinese medicine, live music, Fijian curries, gay club nights, Italian coffee, revival clothing and drag shows. And, like a full stop, at the end of the road are the crumbling gravestones of the Symonds St Cemetery.

INFORMATION

- 🖳 www.kroad.co.nz
- ✉ K Rd, Newton
- 🚌 Link
- 🗙 K Rd (p32)

Its full name is Karangahape Rd, the meaning of which is one of the strip's many mysteries; however, there's a commonly held belief that the name derives from the Maori *'karanga'* (to call on) Hape – an important chief who lived in the Manukau Harbour. History confirms that the K Rd ridge was the Maori's main route to the Manukau Heads. Whatever its origins, 'Karangahape' stuck.

K Rd's solid wall of edifices represents the gamut of architectural styles prevalent during its 60-year reign as the city's busiest shopping hub. Construction of the inner city's scribbled motorway saw the demolition of several thousand buildings in the mid-'60s, resulting in a mighty economic slump. Cheap rents attracted the red-light trade, and a slew of alternative businesses and community centres. K Rd's renaissance really ramped up in the '90s when nightclubs moved in, followed by apartment dwellers. Everyone from businessfolk to artists, musicians and models stop in at this hip, pierced and friendly street.

DON'T MISS

- **Disrupt Gallery** (☎ 369 1540; www.disruptiv.com; 145 K Rd; ☺ 10am-6pm Mon-Fri, 11.30am-3.30 Sat & Sun), which takes Auckland's urban art off-road and indoors
- A top coffee at a K Rd institution: **Alleluya** (p32) or **Brazil** (p32)
- K Rd at night; it's a festival every Friday and Saturday, when crowds spill from the street's drinking dens and dance clubs

Get disrupted at one of K Rd's favourite galleries

AUCKLAND ART GALLERY/TOI O TAMAKI (2, B3)

Playing a prominent part in the Auckland art world, the Auckland Art Gallery is NZ's largest art institution, with around 12,500 works. The permanent collection includes historical paintings – such as embellished urban scenes created to sell early Auckland to potential settlers, and portraits by Charles Goldie – and contemporary pieces: perhaps a palette of kitsch-coloured flowers.

Look out for Brian Brake's photos of a frisky Picasso and Theo Schoon's Maori-inspired observations in nature; the inimitable paintings of John Reynolds and Pat Hanly; and installations by Stella Brennan and Seung Yul Oh. Internationally touring exhibitions also stop in here, such as 'Art & the '60s from Tate Britain'.

In late 2006 the Auckland Art Gallery collection was consolidated into one space – the New Gallery – which previously occupied two sites. The Main Gallery (cnr Wellesley & Kitchener Sts) is having a three-year makeover (it's due to reopen in 2009). The stately French-chateau building (1888) is undergoing earthquake proofing – Auckland sits on a crisscross of fault lines and experiences regular minor murmurs. The gallery is also being expanded to increase its exhibition capacity by 50%, and integrate the space better with its handsome neighbour, Albert Park.

INFORMATION

☎ 307 7700
🖳 www.aucklandartgallery.govt.nz
✉ New Gallery, cnr Wellesley & Lorne Sts
$ admission free; charges apply for special exhibitions
🕑 10am-5pm
🚌 Link
🍴 Reuben

GOLDIE'S OLDIES

Auckland-born Charles Goldie (1870–1947) famously painted elderly Maori. He rendered them in classic European style: with nostalgic lighting and in the finest detail, such that you can see the furrows from chiselled *moko* (tattoos) in wrinkled faces. His sitters are presented with eyes downcast, in despondent and resigned poses. Goldie's representations reflect the widely held European belief of the time (1910s) that Maori culture was in decline – set for assimilation. Today his works fetch the country's highest prices for art, and Maori appreciate his works as links to their ancestors.

AUCKLAND ZOO (3, A3)

Seals, elephants, penguins, cheetahs, meerkats and more are a treat after all those sheep (although the zoo has those too). The coy kiwi makes a 2pm appearance each day at the Native Fauna Encounter, as does the tuatara – a rare reptile (found only in NZ) who's a distant relative to the dinosaur.

INFORMATION

- ☎ 360 3800
- 🖳 www.aucklandzoo.co.nz
- ✉ Motions Rd, Western Springs
- 💲 adult/child $16/8
- 🕥 9.30am-5.30pm
- 🚍 045
- 🍴 café on site

Sure, they *look* cute and fluffy…but have you seen the movie *Gremlins*?

DON'T MISS

- Playing keeper for a day by scrubbing down an elephant or hand feeding a lemur on a Zoom Tour ($60 to $120)
- The elephant paintings: they're no Picasso, but the zoo's elephants have picked up a paintbrush; proceeds from elephant painting sales go to conservation programmes
- The summer series of concerts, when NZ's top musicians perform

Join zoo keepers at scheduled feeding times to see your favourite animal spring into action. This is also the time to ask any burning questions, such as how the spider monkey got its name. The zoo participates in a number of conservation programmes, both in NZ and overseas, and attempts to house its animals in as natural surrounds as possible.

Is it a hedgehog? A pin-cushion? Nanna's feather duster? No, it's a kiwi

KELLY TARLTON'S ANTARCTIC ENCOUNTER & UNDERWATER WORLD (3, C2)

What was previously the city's sewage storage tanks is now, thanks to Kelly Tarlton, a wonderful ocean tunnel teeming with marine life, including sharks, stingrays, fish and other sea critters. Kelly Tarlton was a diver and treasure hunter who used his fortunes (and nous) to invent the ocean tunnel, subsequently installed in aquariums around the world. Be transported to and along the ocean floor, standing on a nifty conveyor belt that runs the length of a giant Perspex tunnel surrounded by a simulated sea. You can also wave at heavyweight Phoebe, the 200kg ray, in the separate stingray enclosure. Sea horses and sea creatures (octopus and eels) have their own separate enclosures.

So too the penguins, which live in the complex's perpetually below-zero Antarctic Encounter section. Ride aboard a heated Snow Cat through a frozen environment where a colony of king and gentoo penguins live. There's also a replica of Scott's 1911 Antarctic hut and displays on the area's history and future.

INFORMATION

- ☎ 528 0603
- 💻 www.kellytarltons.co.nz
- ✉ 23 Tamaki Dr, Orakei
- 💲 adult/child $26/12
- 🕙 9am-6pm
- 🚌 745 to 769, or free shuttle to/from Discover New Zealand (p58; runs hourly 9am-4pm)
- 🅿 free
- 🍴 on-site kiosk

DID YOU KNOW?

- That it's the male sea horses that become pregnant? And (ladies keep laughing) they give birth to between 20 and 400 babies at a time.
- Freshwater eels can't breed in captivity? They require the specific conditions of the sea off the coast of Western Australia to spawn. Poignantly, the adult eels die giving birth, and their young float back to NZ on the currents to start the cycle again.
- King penguins lay only one egg? Which they balance on their feet for the whole incubation period.

Sights & Activities

MUSEUMS & GALLERIES

Auckland's exhibition spaces finally answer the adage: 'if only the walls could talk...' Its many museums and galleries tell much of the city's story, in a vast vocabulary of objects, re-creations and representations. While museums maintain permanent displays, galleries turn over work monthly. *Artzone* (www.artzone.co.nz; $5) is a national directory of galleries detailing what's showing in the city's spaces clustered in the CBD, along Parnell, Ponsonby and K Rds; pick up a copy at newsagents.

Artspace (7, B2)
The plain white walls and concrete floors of this public gallery come to life with an open field of art practices, including sculpture, photography, the moving image and sound art. Artspace exhibits many of New Zealand's leading contemporary artists and promotes a cultural dialogue, both locally and

WALK OF ART
Auckland Art Gallery (p13) publishes a self-guided walking tour that pegs 14 of the city's galleries. They're all free to walk in and between them provide a feast of provocative visual material. Pick up a copy from visitors centres, or download it at www.aucklandartgallery.govt.nz/visit/walkofart/default.asp.

internationally, through speaking programmes and publications.
☎ 303 4965 ▯ www.artspace.org.nz ✉ 300 K Rd, Newton ☯ 10am-6pm Tue-Fri, 11am-4pm Sat 🚌 Link

Artstation (4, A5)
The public gallery of this community arts centre provides a professional space for emerging artists to exhibit their work. Shows turn over every three weeks, and might include contemporary Polynesian themes or those of the modern Goth. If you find the gallery locked, ask the office downstairs for the key.
☎ 376 3221 ▯ www.aucklandcity.govt.nz ✉ 1 Ponsonby Rd, Ponsonby ☯ 9am-5pm Mon-Fri, to 4pm Sat 🚌 Link

John Leech Gallery (2, B3)
At over 150 years old, John Leech Gallery was among the city's first commercial galleries. It represents NZ's most influential, controversial and coveted artists (the likes of Charles Goldie and Theo Schoon).
☎ 303 9395 ▯ www.johnleechgallery.co.nz ✉ cnr Kitchener St & Khartoum Pl, Auckland ☯ 10am-6pm Mon-Fri, 11am-3pm Sat 🚌 Link

Motat (Museum of Transport & Technology) (3, A3)
This unexpected treasure is like being shrunk down to HO size (for nonhobbyists: that's bull-ant sized) and allowed to walk among a train set, model aeroplane collection and Matchbox car rally. They're all real, larger than life and lovingly tended by a small army of ageing volunteers who'll willingly impart first-hand accounts of actually flying or driving these magnificent machines. Entry includes a tram ride from Motat 1 (a Victorian village, automobiles and communications displays) to Motat 2 (planes and trains) — worth the trip.
☎ 0800 668 286, 815 5800 ▯ www.motat.org.nz ✉ Great North Rd, Western Springs $ adult/child $14/7 ☯ 10am-5pm 🚌 045

Motat – where trainspotters go wild

National Maritime Museum (2, B1)
Sea vessels of all shapes, sizes and stages of history are pertinent lessons of the city's connection to the sea. Maori canoes, immigrant ships, jet boats and the old steamboat SS *Puke* will have nautical buffs in knots. Harbour cruises also operate from here.

☎ 0800 725 897, 373 0800 💻 www.nzmaritime.org ✉ cnr Quay & Hobson Sts, Viaduct Harbour 💲 adult/child $12/6 ☺ 9am-6pm Oct-Apr, to 5pm May-Sep 🚌 Link

Oedipus Rex Gallery (2, B3)
Familiar names in the contemporary art world grace this upstairs city space, as do emerging artists working in a variety of forms, including painting, print and photography.

☎ 379 0588 💻 www.orexgallery.co.nz ✉ Upper Khartoum Pl, Kitchener St, Auckland ☺ 11am-5pm Tue-Fri, to 3pm Sat & Mon 🚌 Link

OUTDOOR ACTIVITIES

The region's opportunities to enjoy the great outdoors extend to canyoning, surfing and abseiling (see p25).

Adventure Cycles (2, C2)
This outfit rents road and mountain bikes, with a helmet, lock and maps thrown in. Cycle along Tamaki Dr to Mission Bay, or put the bike on the ferry to Devonport.

☎ 309 5566 💻 www.adventure-auckland.co.nz /adventurecycles ✉ 36

Customs St East, Auckland 💲 half-/full-day hire from $15/20 ☺ 7am-7pm 🚌 Link

Coast to Coast Walkway (3, B4)
This 16km trail links Waitemata and Manukau Harbours, cutting a path through a bunch of sights and attractions such as Auckland Museum and Cornwall Park. Walk one way, then bus back. Pick up a printed copy from visitors centres or download it from the website.

☎ 375 3358 💻 www.aucklandcity.govt.nz/whatson/places/walkways/coasttocoast/map.asp 🚌 328 or 334

Fergs Kayaks (3, B3)
Skate along scenic Tamaki Dr or paddle about the beautiful bay. Go solo or join a guided kayak trip over to Devonport ($75, 8km, 4½ hours).

☎ 529 230 💻 www.fergskayaks.co.nz ✉ 12 Tamaki Dr, Okahu Bay 💲 kayaks per day from $35, in-line skates per day from $30 ☺ 9am-6pm Mon-Fri, 8am-6pm Sat & Sun 🚌 746 or 767 from Britomart

Pride of Auckland (2, B1)
There's a variety of tours guaranteed to put the wind in yer sails, ranging from a short jaunt around the harbour up to a full day with hands-on opportunities to steer her in. Longer tours anchor for lunch, allowing time to swim or wander on a nearby island.

☎ 377 4557 💻 www.prideofauckland.com ✉ National Maritime Museum, cnr Quay & Hobson Sts, Viaduct Harbour 💲 50-minute Sailing Experience adult/child $48/26 ☺ 2.45pm 🚌 Link

Skydive Auckland
Strap yourself to a stranger and jump from a small plane plummeting 5000ft before the bugger pops the chute, and then float the remaining 7000ft to the ground – which you'll then get down and kiss. Includes two-way transport from Auckland.

☎ 0800 865 867, 373 5778 💻 www.skydiveauckland.com ✉ 590 Koheroa Rd, Mercer 💲 tandem $250

BEACHY KEEN
The 28 beaches inside the Auckland isthmus make a big splash with beach-lovers. Popular east-coast beaches along Tamaki Dr include Mission Bay (3, C2) and St Heliers (3, C3). At most east coast and harbour beaches swimming is best at high tide. Popular North Shore beaches include Cheltenham (5, C2) and Takapuna (3, B1).

PARKS & GARDENS

Volcanoes in Auckland are as numerous as pimples on an adolescent. The city's 48 explosive peaks expired centuries ago but left in their wake fertile grounds that are now parkland retreats – often with stellar views.

Albert Park (2, B3)

The giant trees planted here over a century ago have seen it all: student protests, lantern festivals and rock concerts, as well as lots of people lolling in its neat hill-top surrounds. The park was originally a defended *pa* (fortified Maori village), then a barracks, now a cherished city park.
✉ Princes St 🚌 Link

Auckland Botanic Gardens (1, B2)

Opened in 1982, the gardens exhibit youthful exuberance aplenty. Kids love the mythical maze and caterpillar garden. Adults love each other around the formal floral beds for their wedding photographer. Sow the seed of knowledge at the library or plan lunch in the edible garden. And for the weary rambler, the *Wiri Rambler* 'train' scoots between plant collections on weekends.
☎ 267 1457 ✉ Hill Rd, Manurewa ☼ 8am-dusk
🚌 471

Auckland Domain (4, D6)

The gorgeous Domain emanates out from a long-dead volcano: its terraced remains create a natural amphitheatre and a literal level playing field for many sporting grounds.

Stroll through pockets of formal gardens or fringes of bush (on the Parnell side of Domain Dr), and experience perpetual winter at the Wintergarden cool house. The Domain is home to Auckland Museum (p8), a sculpture walk and lots of glorious green space.
✉ main gates, Park Rd, Grafton ☼ sunrise-sunset
🚌 Link

Mt Eden (Maungawhau) (3, B3)

The grassy slopes of Auckland's highest volcanic cone are a popular vantage from which to watch the city and look into the gaping mouth of its crater. Come at dawn to watch the city rise.
✉ 250 Eden Rd, Mt Eden
🚌 274 or 275

One Tree Hill & Cornwall Park (Maungakiekie) (3, B4)

Now two parks, this huge area was once the largest volcanic-cone fortress in the southern hemisphere, said to have

NONE TREE HILL

A sacred totara tree once stood at the top of One Tree Hill before being cut down by a European settler to be used as firewood in 1852. A European-introduced radiata pine was subsequently planted in its place. The tree became a symbol for European dominance over a site with centuries of significance to Maori. The pine was finally felled in 2000. Its questionable stability, resulting in its ultimate demise, came about from chainsaw cuts – as part of two separate Maori protests.

supported up to 5000 Maori; terracing and food-store pits are still visible. The city's European 'father', John Logan Campbell, is buried beneath the big, bald hill alongside the commemorative obelisk. His original house, Acacia Cottage, is in adjacent Cornwall Park. The area's historical significance is explained in the Huia Lodge info centre.
🖳 www.cornwallpark.co.nz
✉ 670 Manukau Rd, Epsom
☼ 7am-dusk 🚌 302, 304, 305 or 312

Parnell Rose Gardens (4, F4)

Watch boats skate across the harbour from this pretty pozzie where you'll be in a bed of blooming roses between November and March. Big old trees, including the oldest manuka in Auckland, watch over the quaint cottagey gardens, which sweep down to the superb saltwater Parnell Baths (p54).
✉ 85-87 Gladstone Rd, Parnell ☼ 7am-7pm
🚌 Link

NOTABLE OLD BUILDINGS

The New Zealand Historic Places Trust (www.historic .org.nz) makes it its mission to maintain the country's heritage buildings. Its restored stately houses, mostly belonging to wealthy pioneer families, have plenty of frills and flounces to help furnish your leap back in time.

Alberton House (3, A3)

The original decorative wallpapers of Alberton House have seen a number of grand balls and music recitals. Sophia Kerr Taylor (widow, mother of 10, singer, gardener and women's-vote advocate) and three of her daughters ran this white timber mansion for around 80 years. More recently, Alberton served as the set for scenes in Jane Campion's award-winning film *The Piano*.
☎ 846 7367 ✉ 100 Mt Albert Rd, Mt Albert $ adult/child $7.50/free ☼ 10.30am-noon & 1-4.30pm Wed-Sun 🚌 230 to 240

Ewelme Cottage (4, E6)

The storybook-cottage metaphor resonates even stronger when you learn the original owners' names: Vicesimus Lush and his wife Blanche. Walking from room to room, filled with books and period pieces, is like turning to another page of polite 19th-century life.
☎ 379 0202 ✉ 14 Ayr St, Parnell $ adult/child $7.50/free ☼ 10.30am-noon & 1-4.30pm Fri-Sun 🚌 328

Highwic (3, B3)

The good china is always out at Highwic, which is finely furnished to reflect the lifestyle of Alfred and Elizabeth Buckland who called it home from around 1862 to 1978. They lived here along with their 21 children (and, no, the house is not shoe shaped).
☎ 524 5729 ✉ 40 Gillies Ave, Epsom; entry via Mortimer Pass $ adult/child $7.50/free ☼ 10.30am-noon & 1-4.30pm Wed-Sun 🚌 290 to 299

Kinder House (4, E6)

The low gabled ceiling of Kinder House shelters a collection of watercolours rendered by the stone cottage's original inhabitant, the Reverend John Kinder. The headmaster of the Church of England grammar school by day and amateur artist by night, Kinder's documentary-style paintings are sensitively observed.
☎ 379 4008 ✉ 2 Ayr St, Parnell $ adult/child $4/1 ☼ 11am-3pm Tue-Sun 🚌 Link

St Mary's Church (4, E5)

The stunning burnished wooden interior and ornate stained-glass windows of the Gothic St Mary's would inspire even atheist aesthetes to attend church. The original commission for a stone church proved too costly, resulting in a wooden St Mary's completed in 1898. In 1982 it was moved across the road to its present position and rotated 90 degrees. The neighbouring **Holy Trinity Cathedral** is where the majority of services are delivered.
☎ 303 9500 🖳 www.holy -trinity.org.nz ✉ Parnell Rd, Parnell ☼ 10am-4pm Mon-Sat, 11am-4pm Sun 🚌 Link

Get pious at St Mary's Church and the Holy Trinity Cathedral

QUIRKY AUCKLAND

Harbour Bridge Bungy & Climb (3, A2)

Auckland is synonymous with superhero-type stunts. Be part of a human chain strung out atop the Harbour Bridge (those strung out by heights need not apply). Or, swan-dive off and dip your nose in the water.

☎ 361 2000 🖳 www .ajhackett.co.nz ✉ West-haven Reserve, Curran St, Auckland 💲 bungy/climb $85/65 🚍 4 or 5

Illicit (7, B2)

If you're looking for a lasting memento of your trip, have an icon etched into your skin at the well-regarded Illicit tattoo studio. If going home with a volcano on your bicep seems too over the top, it does piercing too: specialising in ear stretching, large-gauge and genital jewellery.

☎ 379 2660 🖳 www .illicithq.com ✉ 202 K Rd, Newton 🕑 10am-6pm Mon-Wed, Sat & Sun, to late Thu & Fri 🚍 Link

Lion Breweries (4, D6)

An elaborate excuse to have a drink before 5pm? These two-hour tours include a history of brewing, an audiovisual presentation, a virtual tour of the brewing process and (finally!) some quality time spent sampling Steinlager and Lion Red beers.

☎ 358 8366 🖳 www.lion zone.co.nz ✉ 380 Khy-ber Pass Rd, Newmarket 💲 adult/child $15/7.50 🕑 tours 9.30am, 12.15pm & 3pm Mon-Sat 🚍 Link

Sheepworld

NZ's answer to Disneyland, Sheepworld showcases all things sheepish. Watch working dogs round 'em up on this small farm before feeding the eels in the lake and visiting the gift shop: beauty creme infused with sheep's placenta and 23-carat gold flakes anyone?

☎ 425 7444 🖳 www .sheepworld.co.nz/farm /htm ✉ 324 State Hwy 1, Warkworth 💲 adult/child $16.50/7 🕑 9am-5pm 🚍 SH1 65km north of Auckland

Snowplanet (1, B1)

Every day is a white one at this winter wonderland, with indoor skiing, tobogganing and airboarding. It's five-below in this human-sized snow dome, so rug up.

☎ 427 0044 🖳 www .snowplanet.co.nz ✉ 91 Small Rd, Silverdale 💲 day pass adult/child $60/50 🕑 10am-10pm Sun-Thu, to 11pm Fri & Sat 🚍 SH1 30km north of Auckland

Waikumete Cemetery (1, B2)

The country's largest cemetery is a fascinating historical record, including numerous heritage buildings, plus a South African wild-flower sanctuary. Don't miss the Corban family mauso-leum (they of Corban Wines, once one of NZ's largest and most successful wineries). Guided walks are available on the first Sunday of each month (☎ 817 6547). ✉ Great North Rd, Glen Eden 🕑 7.30am-dusk 🚍 154

AUCKLAND FOR CHILDREN

Auckland's beaches, volcan-oes and parks are excellent playgrounds for little people. And the city's major sights (see Highlights, p8) appeal to travellers of all ages.

Many places run activities for kids during school holi-days (December to Janu-ary, July, and September to October). Check out www .aucklandcity.govt.nz /whatson/kids for pro-gramme details and ideas.

Kids can also benefit from the city's shopping options (p29), with child-friendly books on the region's mythol-ogy, animals and geography, as well as designer duds.

Look for the 🚼 icon listed with individual re-views in the Eating and Sleeping chapters for more kid-friendly options.

Sufferers of vertigo need not apply – Harbour Bridge climb

Scare the kids with spiders, snakes and slimy bugs at Auckland Museum's Discovery Centres

Auckland Museum's Discovery Centres (4, E5)

The museum's children's galleries are the best hands-on learning centres. The Weird & Wonderful gallery has drawers full of spiders, jars full of fish and atriums of scurrying cockroaches, plus microscopes and dress ups a plenty. Treasures & Tales provides insights into everything from woodwork to music.
☎ 306 7067 🖳 www.auck landmuseum.com ✉ Auckland Museum, off Domain Dr, Auckland Domain 💲 free ⏱ 10am-5pm 🚌 Link

Howick Historical Village

Staring at a teddy bear waiting for it to do something brings a whole new love for modern-day 'toys'. Get the kids dressed up for their visit to this 19th-century theme park, with restored buildings staffed by people in period costume.
☎ 576 9506 🖳 www .fencible.org.nz ✉ Bells Rd, Pakuranga 💲 adult/child $12/6 ⏱ 10am-4pm 🚌 51

Parnell Baths (4, F3)

Water babies squeal with delight at the sight of the partly submerged playground here.

Then there's the toddlers' pool with fountains of water squirting from the surrounding wall and the bigger kids' pool. And, there's a café to keep the adults quiet.
☎ 373 3561 ✉ Judges Bay Rd, Parnell 💲 adult/child $5/3 ⏱ 6am-8pm Mon-Fri, 8am-8pm Sat & Sun Nov-Apr 🚌 Link

Rainbow's End

Ride a giant plastic log in a river rapid, lose your stomach in a rocking Pirate Ship or plummet to the ground on the Fear Fall. Kids reckon this is better than the pot of gold at the end of the rainbow.
☎ 262 2030 🖳 www.rain bowsend.co.nz ✉ cnr Great South & Wiri Station Rds, Manukau 💲 unlimited rides adult/child $40/30, spectator $12 ⏱ 10am-5pm 🚌 472 or 478X

Stardome Observatory (3, B4)

Budding astronauts and stargazers will love Stardome's shows, designed for all ages. Screened on a domed ceiling, shows explain everything from how the earth moves to how to measure the universe.
☎ 624 1246 🖳 www.star dome.org.nz ✉ One Tree Hill Domain, off Manukau Rd 💲 adult/child $12/6 ⏱ weekend shows 1.15pm, 2.15pm & 3.15pm 🚌 302-305 & 312

BABYSITTERS

The **Babysitters Company** (☎ 846 3357; www.baby sitterscompany.co.nz) can send over a sitter to look after your little one at the hotel. There's a $15 booking fee, plus a per hour charge between $12 and $14. Alternatively, **Domestic & Service Personnel** (☎ 0800 677 677; www.domestic.co.nz) can locate a sitter, starting at $10 per hour. **Miracles** (4, D4; ☎ 377 3559; www .miracles24hours.co.nz, unit 21/30 Heather St, Parnell) is Auckland's first 'children's hotel', where children can overnight for $150, including meals. There's also a daytime-care option costing $15 per hour (until midnight).

Trips & Tours

WALKING TOURS

Visitors centres and the Department of Conservation (DOC) office have pamphlets detailing walks in and around Auckland. DOC's *Auckland Walkways* pamphlet has a good selection of forest and coastal day walks outside the metropolitan area.

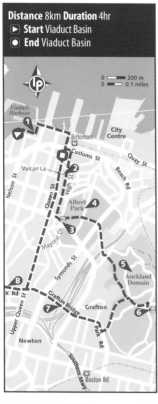

Distance 8km **Duration** 4hr
▶ **Start** Viaduct Basin
◉ **End** Viaduct Basin

Highlights Loop

Say 'hello sailor' in **Viaduct Harbour** (**1**; p9) before walking east along the waterfront and dipping south down High St to **Vulcan Lane** (**2**) and its cluster of cafés. Continue south to **Auckland Art Gallery** (**3**; p13). Then up to **Albert Park** (**4**; p18), originally a fortified Maori village called Rangipuke. Pop out of Albert Park at Alfred St, following it southeast to the **Domain** (**5**; p18), Auckland's Pukekawa (hill of bitter memories – in reference to those killed in the musket wars of the 1820s). The superb **Auckland Museum** (**6**; p8) is also a War Memorial honouring all lives lost in wars.

Go west along Park Rd, crossing **Grafton Bridge** (**7**), touted as the world's biggest span-reinforced concrete-arch bridge at the time it was built (1910). Walk over Upper Queen St, then wander down **K Road** (**8**; p12): Auckland's anything-goes strip, with plenty of shopping opps and gallery stops. Double back down the opposite side, and then make your way north up Queen St back to the waterfront.

Anyone for a game of skittles? Ducks in the Domain (p18)

DAY TRIPS
Rangitoto Island (3, C1)

A mere 600 years ago, the sea in the Hauraki Gulf began to bubble and burst, giving birth to Rangitoto. Rangitoto is now extinct and there's abundant vegetation (some specific to the island) including a sprawling pohutukawa forest (New Zealand Christmas trees, flowering flaming red December–January), plus scrub covering the 260m cinder cone, and wildlife, such as tui birds.

Bring water, food, walking shoes and a swimming costume (or raincoat – weather depending), and hike one of the many walks, a number of which were hand-packed by prisoners in the '20s and '30s. The **summit walk** (two hours return from Rangitoto Wharf) includes a loop around the crater and superb views. A side track on the way up leads to lava caves. From the summit you can continue to the **ships' graveyard** over at Wreck and Boulder Bays (two hours return) – best at low tide. Back at the wharf, a short walk (15 minutes) east passes a bundle of baches (90 years old) and a colony of black-back gulls at Flax Point (one hour). You can also bask on the island's **beaches**: at black-sand McKenzie and Islington Bays. A campground on **Motutapu Island** (1, B1) joins Rangitoto by causeway.

INFORMATION
10km northeast of central Auckland

- 🚢 Fullers from Auckland's Ferry Bldg: adult/child return $19/11
- 🖥 www.doc.govt.nz
- ℹ DOC information centre (☎ 379 6476; aucklandvc@doc.govt.nz; ground fl, Ferry Bldg, Quay St; ☯ 9.30am-5pm Mon-Fri & 10am-3pm Sat Oct–Easter)

Sail away, sail away, sail away…to Rangitoto Island

Waitakere Ranges & Western Beaches (1, A2)

Waitakere Ranges Regional Park is bordered to the west by wildly beautiful beaches, and the park's sometimes rugged terrain and steep-sided valleys are squiggled with 250km of **walking trails**. Amble up to waterfalls or tramp for hours through coast and country. A number of shorter trails leading from **Titirangi's** impressive info and educative centre, **Arataki visitors centre**, are suitable for wheelchairs and prams.

Waitakere is also on the **wine trail**, with many premium producers' products speaking for themselves at cellar-door tastings. The free *Winemakers of Auckland* brochure details local wineries, many with excellent eateries attached.

Along the west coast there are rugged, wind-lashed beaches. Swimmers splash about between lifesavers' flags, and surfers compete at the iron-sand **Piha Beach**, which has a path out to the distinctive offshore **Lion Rock**. Continue north to beautiful black-sand **Te Henga** (Bethells Beach) and up to Muriwai Beach, with its 4000-strong **colony of gannets** (between August and March).

INFORMATION

20km west from central Auckland to Arataki visitors centre

- State Hwy 16 west. Take Exit 2 onto Great North Rd to Titirangi.
- Auckland Regional Parks (www.arc.govt.nz) & Waitakere City Council (www.waitakere.govt.nz)
- Arataki visitors centre (☎ 366 2000; info@arc.govt.nz; Scenic Dr, Titirangi; ☼ 9am-5pm Sep-Apr, to 4pm May-Aug)

Waiheke Island (1, C1)

This island in the Hauraki Gulf boasts rolling farmland, forest, vineyards and olive groves. The generally creative community of 8500 watches its island paradise become inundated by 10,000 summer-holidaying Aucklanders each year. They travel the short distance (40 minutes) for a taste of island life, surrounded by picturesque bays protecting swimming **beaches** and stunning coastal and bush **walks**. Over 30 **artists' studios** are open to visitors,

PISSED PIGEONS

You can't miss NZ's native wood pigeon (called *kereru* or *kukupa* in Maori). The whoosh of wings from these large white-vested grey/green feathered birds is a much-loved sound heard in low-lying bush, such as Waitakere. Recent reports have expressed concern for the *kereru*, which are getting drunk from eating fermented guava. Not a bad thing in itself, except flying under the influence has resulted in large numbers meeting an untimely end by crashing into cars and windows. As the last surviving species large enough to digest and disperse seeds from large fruited trees, the declining numbers of *kereru* could spell the end of these bush areas as we know them.

and 24 **wineries** (www.waihekewine.co.nz) – many with flash restaurants attached – are open for tastings. See the lot by driving the **scenic loop road** at the east end of the island.

Waiheke features a number of settlements – the main one is **Oneroa** – as well as an established infrastructure, including a proliferation of accommodation, transport, tours and activities.

INFORMATION
18km east from central Auckland
- from Auckland's Ferry Bldg adult/child $26/13, from Half Moon Bay (1, B2) adult/child/car $26.50/14.50/113
- www.tourismwaiheke.co.nz
- Waiheke Island visitors centre (☎ 372 1234; info@waiheke.co.nz; 2 Koroa Rd, Oneroa; 9am-5pm)

Arrive at Waiheke Island in style

ORGANISED TOURS

Awol Canyoning
Abseil into waterfalls, jump into canyons and wade through glow-worm caves in the Waitakere Ranges. Or bask on the black sand after boogie boarding at Piha Beach. Pick-up from Auckland and snacks are included, and there are different levels of physical activity to suit all abilities. Half-day tours are also available.
☎ 834 0501 www.awol adventures.co.nz $ full day $155 9.30am-5pm

Fullers Cruises (2, B1)
Fullers' Harbour Cruise takes in Devonport, the Harbour Bridge and Viaduct Harbour. It includes commentary, coffee and a cookie. Fullers also operates a variety of good-value combination transport-and-tour options to a number of islands in the gulf, including Waiheke and Rangitoto.
☎ 367 9111 www.ful lers.co.nz Ferry Bldg, Quay St $ 1½hr cruise adult/child $31/16 cruises 10.30am & 1.30pm

NZ Surf Tours
Always wanted to wear a rubber suit and experience the closest thing to walking on water? Make it easy on yourself by taking a tour, with big spongy boards (read: easy-to-ride), wet suits and lessons (optional) included. Five-day tours chase the waves, and include transport, accommodation and food.
☎ 828 0426 www.new zealandsurftours.com $ day/5-day tours $100/700 Oct–Jun

Potiki Adventures
These Maori-run tours for small groups could easily amount to one of your favourite Auckland days. Choose from the Urban Maori tour, which includes One Tree Hill, Otara Market, Waitakere and a wildly beautiful west-coast beach, or the Marine Reserve kayaking tour.
☎ 845 5932 www.potiki adventures.com $ Urban Maori $145, Marine Reserve $185

Wine Trail Tours
This tastings tour calls in at your choice of five wineries in Waitakere, and includes a scenic drive along the wild west coast to Muriwai's gannet colony. The tour includes a winery lunch.
☎ 630 1540 www.wine trailtours.co.nz $ $150 10am-5pm

Shopping

Like any big city, Auckland has a healthy commercial heart. Aucklanders produce and value quality goods, but they wouldn't be caught dead wearing a sheepskin hat like those lining the shelves of souvenir shops. You will find them wearing internationally coveted clothes made locally by Auckland's multitude of clever designers. The city's fresh and prepared produce is nothing to sniff at either. Auckland's renowned wines make a fabulous memento. Other easy-to-come-by Kiwiana includes items inlaid with paua shell, greenstone (*pounamu*) jewellery, garments made from a blend of wool and possum fur, plus sheepskin, sheepskin and sheepskin.

There are sales at the start of each season, with post-Christmas being the biggest sale time. Most shops accept major credit cards; markets are cash based. For opening hours, see p57.

TOP SPOTS TO SHOP
- High St, central Auckland (2, B2): high-end fashion
- K Rd, Newton (7, A2): from quirky to couture
- Ponsonby Rd, Ponsonby (8, B2): chichi chic
- New North Rd, Kingsland (6, A2): excellent eclectic goods

Don't let life get you down at Misery

CLOTHING & SHOE SIZES

Women's Clothing
Aust/UK	8	10	12	14	16	18
Europe	36	38	40	42	44	46
Japan	5	7	9	11	13	15
USA	6	8	10	12	14	16

Women's Shoes
Aust/USA	5	6	7	8	9	10
Europe	35	36	37	38	39	40
France only	35	36	38	39	40	42
Japan	22	23	24	25	26	27
UK	3½	4½	5½	6½	7½	8½

Measurements approximate only; try before you buy.

Men's Clothing
Aust	92	96	100	104	108	112
Europe	46	48	50	52	54	56
Japan	S	M	M		L	
UK/USA	35	36	37	38	39	40

Men's Shirts (Collar Sizes)
Aust/Japan	38	39	40	41	42	43
Europe	38	39	40	41	42	43
UK/USA	15	15½	16	16½	17	17½

Men's Shoes
Aust/UK	7	8	9	10	11	12
Europe	41	42	43	44½	46	47
Japan	26	27	27.5	28	29	30
USA	7½	8½	9½	10½	11½	12½

CLOTHES & JEWELLERY

Fingers (2, B3)

This gallery-cum-shop has precious objects designed and crafted by around 50 local jewellers. Individual pieces may reference nature, New Zealand icons and identity. Materials used include precious metals, shells, fabrics, stone and found objects. Fingers has been around for over 30 years, and hosts regular solo and group shows. ☎ 373 3974 🖳 www .fingers.co.nz ✉ 2 Kitchener St, Auckland 🕑 10am-5.30pm Mon-Fri, to 4.30pm Sat 🚇 Link

Hailwood (7, A3)

Ladies and gentlemen no longer have to pick through other boutiques' racks looking for popular local designer Adrian Hailwood's smart and playful pieces; they're all consolidated here in his own-label store. (Sometimes you'll find him here too, working out the back!) Expect 'his' and 'hers' shirts and jumpers made from silk or velvet fabrics with a juvenile-retro woodland print, or classic '50s cuts in Western fabrics. ☎ 360 9931 🖳 www.hail wood.co.nz ✉ 516 K Rd, Newton 🚇 Link

Karen Walker (2, B2)

Internationally coveted designer Karen Walker's pieces give a nod both ways: to streetwear and to tailoring. Her name is now on everything from sunglasses to house paint. ☎ 309 6299 🖳 www .karenwalker.com ✉ 15 O'Connell St, Auckland 🚇 Link

Little Brother (2, B2)

One for the fellows, Little Brother has its own line of streetwear. Designs are created and made in NZ. Also in store, look for T-shirts emblazoned by iconic music label Flying Nun, and miniature Little Brother pieces for boys (aged one to eight) under the Little Shit label. ☎ 377 6536 🖳 www .littlebrotheronline.com ✉ 5 High St, Auckland 🚇 Link

Misery (7, B2)

She started on the street, spraying twisted cutesy motifs about town. Then Misery's work moved in to galleries (fetching $2500) and grew to her own boutique. The paintings are still for sale, but are now surrounded by a range of bags, shirts, hoodies, T-shirts and small smalls. ☎ 302 2504 🖳 www .miseryboutique.com ✉ 202 K Rd, Newton 🚇 Link

Royal Jewellery Studio (6, A2)

Royal presents a vast array of the country's finest ornamentation. From traditional *pounamu* pieces imbued with *karakia* (Maori incantations and prayers) from artists such as Te Kaha to Joanna Campbell's pieces referencing dressmaking. The studio is housed in the fittingly dramatic Art Deco building of the former Royal Theatre. ☎ 846 0200 🖳 www .royaljewellerystudio.com ✉ 486 New North Rd, Kingsland 🕑 10am-6pm Mon-Fri, to 4pm Sat, to 2pm Sun 🚉 Kingsland

Wunderkammer (8, C3)

High-end imports such as Costume National mix in with locally designed accessories and the occasional stuffed animal. Personable and idiosyncratic, Wunderkammer is an experience, not just a shop. ☎ 360 4090 ✉ 76a Ponsonby Rd, Ponsonby 🚇 Link

Zambesi (8, B3)

Hands-down the most influential and interesting fashion label to come out of the country. Zambesi's twisted classics are strikingly unique, crafted to last and internationally renowned. A second store is located in the city (2, B1; ☎ 303 1701; cnr Vulcan Lane & O'Connell St) ☎ 360 4953 🖳 www.zam besi.co.nz ✉ 169 Ponsonby Rd, Ponsonby 🚇 Link

MARKETS

Aotea Sq Market (4, B4)

Aotea Sq is transformed into a tent city, with around 90 stalls pedalling locally made wares. Expect clothing, jewellery, and arts and crafts such as ethnic-inspired oils or accessories. Fuel up at food stalls and dig the free entertainment on Saturday afternoon. ✉ Aotea Sq 🕑 10am-6pm Fri & Sat 🚇 Link

Auckland Fish Market
(4, A2)
Catch boisterous early-morning auction action, plus plenty of retailers and a cooking school where you can learn to cook your catch (or purchase).
☎ 379 1490 🖳 www .aucklandfishmarket.co.nz ✉ cnr Jellicoe & Daldy Sts ⊗ 7am-7pm 🚌 Link

Otara Market (3, D5)
Punters come before sunrise for the Polynesian flavours. A sprawl of stalls stock prepared South Pacific foods, music and fashions, plus fruit and veg. A great place to find authentic flaxware, T-shirts and jewellery, without the city price tags.
☎ 274 0830 ✉ Newbury St, Otara ⊗ 6am-noon Sat 🚌 487 or 497

Takapuna Market (3, B1)
Locals buzz around stalls laden with fruit and veg, plants and flowers, and prepared foods. Make a day of it: dining at a nearby café and heading down to the beach or along the two-hour Takapuna–Milford Heritage Walk, which passes a fossilized forest.
✉ central car park, Anzac St, Takapuna ⊗ 6am-noon Sun 🚌 839 or 879

Victoria Park Market
(4, A3)
Once a rubbish dump, Victoria Park is now the repository for clothes, shoes, crafts and souvenirs. It includes a food court, spacious pub and clutch of cafés. Cheap massages are available and there's live entertainment on weekends.
☎ 309 6911 🖳 www .victoria-park-market.co.nz ✉ 210 Victoria St W, Auckland ⊗ 9am-6pm 🚌 Link

BOOKS & MUSIC

Marbecks (2, B2)
This long-established music supplier stocks all genres, including NZ-made and children's (such as *Baby Jazz*, and albums by 'Bratz', NZ's number-one selling doll). You'll find classics, country and hip-hop too.
☎ 379 0444 🖳 www .marbecks.co.nz ✉ Queens Arcade, Auckland 🚌 Link

Real Groovy (7, C1)
Either come knowing what you want or with a lot of spare time – should you find yourself lost in this behemoth store's sea of CDs, vinyl, books, games, clothes and DVDs.
☎ 302 3940 🖳 www .realgroovy.co.nz ✉ 438 Queen St, Auckland ⊗ 9am-9pm Mon-Sat, to 7pm Sun 🚌 Link

Unity Books (2, B2)
These well-stocked shelves contain books from every genre, but Unity specialises in locally published works and the cream of international imports. Check out the 'staff recommendations' shelves, with helpful hand-written reviews to guide you.
☎ 307 0731 🖳 www .unitybooks.co.nz ✉ 19 High St, Auckland 🚌 Link

Whitcoulls (2, B3)
Your run-of-the-mill big bookshop, Whitcoulls is where you can anonymously flick through magazines, and scan the shelves for self-help titles, airport reads and a selection of NZ literature.
☎ 356 5400 🖳 www .whitcoulls.co.nz ✉ 210 Queen St, Auckland 🚌 Link

LOOKY HERE & LISTEN UP

Novels, poems and short stories written by Aucklanders abound: look for literature by Janet Frame, CK Stead, Tina Shaw and Frank Sargeson. For smart commentary on Auckland's food, arts and politics read *Metro* magazine.

A CD by local lyricist Lorina Harding would make a stellar soundtrack to any Auckland trip, as would NZ's other leading lady Bic Runga. Keep an ear out for the skewed classic pop/rock of SJD and the legendary Fats White, headed by the ever-provocative Brent Hayward. And don't miss sampling Mark de Clive-Lowe's jazz, funk and soul beats.

Something to suit everyone's taste at Marbecks

FOR CHILDREN

Adopt an Animal (3, A3)
What better present to buy than a rhino? Even better, it stays where it is: at the zoo. Adopting a NZ threatened species, such as a kiwi, kokako, kaka or tuatara, lasts for one year and supports the zoo's conservation efforts.
☎ 360 3800 ☐ www .aucklandzoo.co.nz ✉ Auckland Zoo, Motions Rd, Western Springs ⌚ 9.30am-5.30pm 🚌 045

Children's Bookshop
(8, B1)
Chock-a-block with stories, adventures and education titles. The excellent NZ section stocks supreme children's authors such as Margaret Mahy and Pamela Allen, as well as Maori myths. Helpful staff.
☎ 376 7283 ☐ www .childrensbookshop.co.nz ✉ cnr Jervois & St Marys Rds, Ponsonby 🚌 Link

Hive of Activity (3, B3)
Every variety of game and toy is guaranteed by friendly staff who have road-tested the lot. This colourful shop is stocked full of little plastic farm animals, board games, dress-ups and other fun things like Slinky and Silly Putty.
☎ 623 1181 ✉ 377 Manukau Rd, Epsom 🚌 348 or 502

Kaf Kids (8, A1)
Pint-sized designer clothes in boho styles for little dahling girls and boys. T-shirts, tops, jackets and dresses, plus hats and accessories are all imagined and made locally from durable pre-shrunk cottons.
☎ 360 8131 ✉ 85 Jervois Rd, Ponsonby 🚌 Link

Buy something black from Champions of the World

MADE IN NZ

Buana Satu (7, B2)
Kitschy tea towels and chilli-pepper fairy lights mix in with woven flax bags, baskets and jewellery. Clothing, tin toys and leis make other great buys.
☎ 358 5561 ✉ 229 K Rd, Newton 🚌 Link

Champions of the World
(2, B2)
Pick up a Rugby Union hat or T-shirt. Only problem is, official merchandise comes in one colour: All Blacks. Great retro one-day cricket gear worn by the Black Caps also available.
☎ 379 4937 ☐ www .champions.co.nz ✉ 22 Queen St, Auckland 🚌 Link

Native Agent (6, A2)
Handmade heirlooms reference Maori and colonial history. Buy a quilt, jewellery or picture designed by local artist Rona Ngahuia Osborne and friends. Embroidered shirts and linens are gorgeous.
☎ 845 3289 ☐ www .nativeagent.co.nz ✉ 507b New North Rd, Kingsland ☒ Kingsland

Pauanesia (2, B3)
This colourful little shop stocks souvenirs and gifts with Polynesian style. Exotic items include handmade paper products and *kete* (woven-flax bag and basketware).
☎ 366 7282 ✉ 35 High St, Auckland 🚌 Link

Eating

Auckland's size and ethnic diversity put it at the top of the food chain: in possession of the country's best range of eateries. The superb quality of New Zealand produce provides the advantage in city menus' superior dishes. And partnered with a stellar local sauv blanc, dining out in Auckland is a serious highlight.

Descending on Vulcan Lane for a feed

An enviable position, nestled between two harbours, informs Auckland's partiality for seafood. Green-lipped mussels are a Kiwi icon – made more so by their healing anti-inflammatory properties. Scrutinise a top-notch menu for paua (abalone), and keep an eye out for always-good whitebait. It's hardly surprising that lamb features on most menus; roast lamb or hogget (an animal over 12 months old) comprise part of the average family meal. Pacific and Asian influences materialise in many menus, in the guise of Pacific Rim cookery.

There are loads of diverse restaurant options throughout the city, most open for lunch (noon to 3pm) and dinner (6pm to 10pm). There's also an abundance of cafés that serve breakfast and lunch (often counter service), and sometimes dinner – many serving all day from 8am. Tipping for good service is always appreciated. A 15% to 20% restaurant surcharge applies on public holidays.

Exceptionally good coffee fuels the café set, with stylish fit outs and pavement seating. Restaurants and cafés are smoke-free, most offer a veg option or more and the majority of cafés welcome children. (Generally, ethnic eateries are particularly child- and veg-friendly.) Weekends are busy at cafés, with locals indulging in a cooked café breakfast. Weekdays, Aucklanders'll generally start the day with cereal, fruit or toast. Lunch is usually bread based, and eaten from a paper bag at the desk, on the street or at the park without any pomp or ceremony, unless it's a special occasion. The main meal, dinner, takes place any time between 6pm and 9pm.

CITY CENTRE

Cafe Melba (2, B2)
Cafe $$
Old school dim and moody café with businessfolk clustered at teeny tables both inside and out. At breakfast, there is eggs Benedict done three ways: veg, regular and with salmon. Or dip your spoon in delectable stewed fruit or porridge. Later at lunch, the menu moves to bagels and curries.
☎ 377 0091 ✉ 33 Vulcan Lane ☾ breakfast & lunch 🚌 Link ♿

Mentatz (2, B3)
Japanese & Korean $$
Japanese and Korean faves for homesick students dominate Mentatz' long menu. The atmosphere is low-key and friendly, and the bill is always small. Try the spicy cold *ramen* (noodles), which is true to its title, or some *shiokara* (squid marinated in its own guts).
☎ 357 0960 ✉ 28 Lorne St ☾ lunch Mon-Fri, dinner daily 🚌 Link

O'Connell Street Bistro (2, B2)
Sophis bistro $$$$
The delightful bistro has elegant décor and wonderful food and wine. Its 12 tables satisfy lunchtime businesspeople and dinnertime daters. The Eurocentric menu leans heavily on the duck, salmon and lamb side of things.
☎ 377 1884 🖥 www.oconnellstbistro.com ✉ 3 O'Connell St ☾ lunch Tue-Fri, dinner Mon-Sat 🚌 Link

Sheinkin (2, B3)
Israeli inspired $$
All those light bulbs hanging above your head confirm the idea of coming here as a good one. This minimalist, white-space place lends an arty air to the suited CBD, and does stellar tasting plates, soups and salads. Stacks of glossy reading material await to join you for a perfect brew.
☎ 303 4301 ✉ 3 Lorne St ☾ breakfast & lunch 🚌 Link

Toto (2, A3)
Italian $$$
A comprehensive list of Italian and NZ wines accompanies Toto's choice of fine Italian fare. And dinner ain't over in the Montecristo Room till the fat lady sings, with set menu and opera singing available Saturday. Movie and music nights also feature.
☎ 302 2665 🖥 www.toto restaurant.co.nz ✉ 53 Nelson St ☾ lunch Mon-Fri, dinner daily 🚌 Link

The sassy White Lady serves up a top burger

White Lady (2, B2)
Burger bus $$
The lady in white stealthily materialises after dark, or is it that everyone's too drunk to notice her arrive? This mobile burger bus has been frying up fast food to late-night boozers since the '50s. The burgers are exxy, but monstrous and greasy and best enjoyed while bathed in the neon glow of the late-night city.
✉ Shortland St ☾ 7.30pm-3am Mon-Thu, 24hr Fri-Sun 🚌 Link

EAT STREETS

- Vulcan Lane, High Stand Lorne St: small, smart, city-centre cafés
- Ponsonby Rd: hip, sceney bar and restaurant strip
- Parnell Rd: compact and refined
- The Viaduct and Princes Wharf: heaving weekend waterfront action

THE VIADUCT & PRINCES WHARF

Euro (2, B1)
Mod NZ $$$$

The oft-lauded Euro holds a few surprises. Its sleek and sparse dining space belies its buzzy atmosphere and adventurous path taken by the kitchen. Euro's menu makes forays into molecular gastronomy, with mains featuring foams, wafers, jellies and jams. Made from superior local produce, the tastes and textures achieved are a true dining-out treat. ☎ 309 9856 🖳 www.the nourishgroup.co.nz/eurobar ✉ Shed 22, Princes Wharf 🕑 lunch & dinner 🖩 Link

Soul (2, A1)
Seafood restaurant $$$$

Like interactive dining, at Soul you match your chosen fish variety with one of five available preparations. Always-attentive waiters will recommend the perfect local wine to partner it, or one of the many meat and veg options also available. Despite its large size, it really packs 'em in. And you know a place is popular when it sells its own merchandise. ☎ 356 7249 🖳 www.soul bar.co.nz ✉ Viaduct Harbour 🕑 brunch Sat & Sun, lunch & dinner daily 🖩 Link

White (4, C2)
High-end hotel restaurant $$$$

Perfectly propped high above Waitemata Harbour, White's gleaming interior reflects nature's mood. Terrace tables are a treat in fine weather, and the stretched communal table makes a comfy landing for solo diners. Fine local produce is treated with cooking styles and ingredients from around the world, and partnered with international and local wines. Bookings essential. ☎ 978 2000 🖳 www .whiterestaurant.co.nz ✉ Hilton Hotel, Princes Wharf 🕑 breakfast, lunch & dinner 🖩 Link

Wildfire (2, B1)
Brazilian barbecue $$$

This is dramatic dining with an all-you-can-eat element. Tell your knife-wielding *passador* (waiter) when you can eat no more of the giant skewers of meat, otherwise they'll keep coming with more marinated lamb, beef, fish or sausages sliced straight to the plate. There's a small à la carte menu too. ☎ 353 7595 🖳 www.wild firerestaurant.co.nz ✉ Princes Wharf 🕑 lunch & dinner 🖩 Link ♿

Wildfire: all-you-can-eat yum

K ROAD

Alleluya (7, B2)
Café $$

Like the funky uncle of the K Rd community, Alleluya has been serving up great grub seasoned with humour for a decade. Take a table out in the arcade and toy with the avocado and croutons in your '80s mixed salad. Views over Myers Park are equally delicious, and you can drop in for drinks Thursday to Saturday when it stays open late. ☎ 377 8424 ✉ 13-14 St Kevins Arcade, K Rd 🕑 breakfast & lunch daily, dinner Tue-Sat 🖩 Link ♿

Brazil (7, B2)
Café $$

Boho Brazil café's exposed plumbing and peeling paint would make Terry Gilliam proud. Serious coffee drinkers are also proud of Brazil's home-roast brew from beans prepared in the basement. Filled bagels and great breakfasts are served amongst electro-industrial soundscapes and aromas of steaming coffee. ☎ 302 2677 ✉ 256 K Rd 🕑 breakfast & lunch 🖩 Link

Caluzzi (7, A2)
Dinner 'n' show $$

Would you like drag with your steak? Your three-course set meal ($50) comes with lashings of torch-song tunes, repartee and cheek (both buttocks and behavioural varieties) delivered by your drag queen-diva waitresses. Best you book a babysitter and book ahead. ☎ 357 0778 🖳 www .caluzzi.co.nz ✉ 461 K Rd 🕑 dinner Tue-Sat 🖩 Link

Caluzzi has the classiest drag queen waitresses

Le Petit Bouchon (7, B2)
Creperie $$

Simply French in a quintessentially K Rd location, this *petit* café serves bucket-sized café au lait – the traditional way. Crepe aromas and French accents escape from its little doors to join the hubbub of St Kevins Arcade. More sedate at night, when you can settle in with a big glass of red and crepe for main and dessert.
☎ 379 9144 ✉ 6/183 St Kevins Arcade, K Rd ⏲ lunch daily, dinner Thu-Sat ⛟ Link

Satya (7, B2)
South Indian $$

Sometimes you just need a home-cooked meal, and sometimes it's even better when it doesn't actually come from your home. Satya's simple, spicy South Indian food is lighter than most Indian, and offers lots of veg and vegan dishes. Satya is a popular local haunt.
☎ 377 0007 ✉ 271 K Rd ⏲ lunch Mon-Sat, dinner daily ⛟ Link ♿

Verona (7, B3)
Café $$

This lush and loved eatery serves mostly organic food to diners ensconced in booths. Dishes on the pert Eur-Asian menu cross continents, such as the spaghetti with roast chicken and bok choy tossed with chilli, Vietnamese mint and basil.
☎ 307 0508 ⌨ www .verona.co.nz ✉ 169 K Rd ⏲ brunch & lunch Mon-Sat, dinner daily ⛟ Link

Relive the food of the '80s at Alleluya

PARNELL

Antoines (4, E5)
Fine French $$$$
Ring the doorbell of this villa-style restaurant to alert the waiters of your arrival. The last word in old-fashioned fine dining, it offers a supplementary 'nostalgia' menu, featuring favourites from its early days in the '70s.
☎ 379 8756 🖳 www.antoinesrestaurant.co.nz ✉ 333 Parnell Rd 🕙 lunch Wed-Fri, dinner Mon-Sat 🚌 Link

Iguacu (4, E5)
Pacific-Rim restaurant $$$
Popular multilevel bar and restaurant offering smart, casual dining. The menu is meat heavy, with a smattering of seafood. The relaxed atmosphere heats up on Sunday afternoon with live blues and jazz.
☎ 358 4804 🖳 www.iguacu.co.nz ✉ 269 Parnell Rd 🕙 breakfast Sat & Sun, lunch & dinner daily 🚌 Link

Java Room (4, E5)
Asian $$
Java Room is full of delicious contradictions: its dishes are

Go upmarket at Antoines

subtle yet complex, with Asian accents served in elegant Euro surrounds. Surprisingly affordable for the quality.
☎ 366 1606 🖳 www.javaroom.co.nz ✉ 317 Parnell Rd 🕙 dinner Mon-Sat 🚌 Link

Oh Calcutta (4, E4)
Indian $$
Arguably the country's best Indian (they will argue), Oh Calcutta ventures beyond the familiar butter chicken into exotic and ebullient menu territory. Try the sweet chilli duck, fish tikka (spiced and smoked) or something from the tandoor.
☎ 377 9090 🖳 www.ohcalcutta.co.nz ✉ 151 Parnell Rd 🕙 lunch Wed-Fri, dinner daily 🚌 Link ♿

FOR THE LOVE OF PAVLOVA

In what could be the world's biggest food fight, for over 70 years both New Zealanders and Australians have claimed the pavlova as their national dish. The iconic meringue cake is named after Anna Pavlova, the ballerina whose fluffy white skirts shared light and white attributes with the cake. Pavlova's biographer, plus the existence of a number of recipes from the '20s, points to the pav being invented in NZ. Though there is evidence to suggest that the Aussies improved on, then named, NZ's meringue cake. In NZ, the pav is usually topped with kiwi fruit – in case you were in any doubt as to its origins.

PONSONBY

Agnes Curran (7, B2)
Cool home-style café $$
Beyond the courtyard, this café embodies the kind of homely comforts that encourage staying a while. A homemade melting moment or lamington with tea or coffee tastes better surrounded by vintage-style kitchen gear and pottery. There are also quiches, pies and filled baguettes.
☎ 360 1551 ✉ 181 Ponsonby Rd 🕙 breakfast & lunch 🚌 Link

Bonita (7, B2)
Tapas $$
Share a plate of tasty morsels, with a great glass of wine. The blackboard is scrawled with specials and the distressed walls carry shelves stacked with Spanish produce.
☎ 376 5670 ✉ 242 Ponsonby Rd 🕙 dinner Tue-Sun 🚌 Link

Dizengoff (7, B2)
Café $$
This gleaming high-turnover café takes a sparse approach: its white theme extending to the whiteboard of few words. The dishes speak for themselves: 'mushrooms on toast' means button mushrooms in smooth gravy spiked with paprika and pesto on sourdough.
☎ 360 0108 ✉ 256 Ponsonby Rd 🕙 breakfast & lunch 🚌 Link

Logos (8, B1)
Very veg café $$
Space Age meets New Age at Logos café. With low-slung lightbulbs downstairs and themed rooms upstairs (brought to you by the

BUSINESS OR PLEASURE?

About to seal that all-important deal over dinner? It may be good to know that the restaurant your friend raved about does drag at Friday lunch. Following are a few suggestions to avoid any awkward Auckland dining experiences.

Best Business

For smart surrounds and service, try O'Connell Street Bistro (p31) or Soul (p32).

It's All About the View

It has to be **Orbit** (2, A3; ☎ 363 6000; Sky Tower), perched 300-odd metres up Sky Tower.

Very Veg

Auckland's multitude of multiethnic have meat-free dishes: try Satya (p33), Logos (p34) or Mekong Neua (p36).

Going Solo

Cafés are always casual and plumb for one. Try Dizengoff (p34), Santos (below) or Sheinkin (p31), all with stacks of mags to keep you company.

colour blue, green and one Mid-East–inspired). The mostly veg menu sneaks in some chicken and seafood, but offers lots of animal-free dishes. It's all healthy, though not so healthy as to eschew booze.

☎ 376 2433 🖳 www.cafe logos.com ✉ 265 Ponsonby Rd 🕑 breakfast & lunch Wed-Mon, dinner daily 🚍 Link

Rocco (8, C3)
Spanish style $$$
Here, your glass will likely be filled with a heady mix from the cocktail list, and you'll be toasting the flamboyant and friendly service that brings you exceptionally fine Spanish-accented fare.

☎ 360 6262 🖳 www .rocco.co.nz ✉ 23 Ponsonby Rd 🕑 lunch Mon-Fri, dinner Mon-Sat 🚍 Link

Santos (8, C3)
Café $$
Kicker coffee keeps Ponsonby types familiar with the person driving the machine. Pastries and breakfast (served til 3pm) in the courtyard are a local ritual.

☎ 378 8431 ✉ 114 Ponsonby Rd 🕑 breakfast & lunch 🚍 Link

SPQR (8, B3)
Italian $$$
Dress up for this hot spot, well known for Roman-style thin-crust pizza. If you want to up the ante, select snapper (baked, with salty trimmings). The surrounds are stylish and the staff have all the smooth moves. Book ahead.

☎ 360 1710 ✉ 150 Ponsonby Rd 🕑 lunch & dinner daily 🚍 Link

DEVONPORT

Esplanade Restaurant
(5, A3)
Hotel restaurant $$$ & Café $$
The fairly conservative restaurant menu (lamb shanks and chargrilled salmon) is in contrast to the outrageously good location: a corner commanding harbour views. The hotel's **Mecca café** (🕑 breakfast, lunch and dinner) offers a more casual alternative, with more menu options than the restaurant, including egg-based and sweet dishes for brekky or brunch.

☎ 445 1291 🖳 www .esplanadehotel.co.nz ✉ 1 Victoria Rd 🕑 lunch Tue-Sun, dinner Tue-Sat, brunch Sat & Sun 🚢 Devonport

Enjoy more than just great food at the Esplanade Restaurant (p35)

Manuka (5, A3)
Pacifica $$$
Bumper breakfasts and pizza cooked how it should be – fuelled by wood. Snaffle the corner window booth to watch the passing traffic or hover over a sprawling weekend paper.
☎ 445 7732 ☐ www.manukarestaurant.co.nz ✉ 49 Victoria Rd ☺ breakfast Sat & Sun, lunch & dinner daily 🚇 Devonport ♿

Monsoon (5, A3)
Thai/Malaysian $$
Monsoon is a low-key local. Come with a rabble of friends or on your lonesome for zingy curries and saucy mains. Monsoon does BYO and takeaway.
☎ 445 4263 ✉ 71 Victoria Rd ☺ dinner 🚇 Devonport ♿

Stone Oven (5, A3)
Bakery café $$
So damn good that on weekends you'll want to get in early or get ready to queue at the counter groaning under the weight of cakes, breads and pies. Sweet- and savoury-tooths are sated at breakfast: banana and ricotta pancakes with passionfruit for sweeties, and garlic mushies with parmesan and basil on sourdough for savoury savourers. Lunchers fill up on substantial salads, a burger or pasta dish.
☎ 445 3185 ✉ 5 Clarence St ☺ breakfast & lunch 🚇 Devonport ♿

Zigana (5, A3)
Med-inspired café $$
Owner Ramazan Semiz is everyone's friend. Tuck into a house-roast coffee or Mod-NZ main of chicken, lamb or fish. Thin-crust pizzas promise the world, with toppings from Alaska, Greece, Sicily and (not least) Turkey – spiced lamb, butter, parsley and fresh tomato.
☎ 445 4151 ☐ www.ziganaespresso.com ✉ 46 Victoria Rd ☺ breakfast, lunch & dinner 🚇 Devonport ♿

KINGSLAND

Canton Cafe (6, B2)
Chinese $$
Constant queues outside Canton Cafe's door are a sign of the popularity of this BYO-wine place's excellent Chinese dishes, which you'll have done and dusted within 30 minutes. Next!
☎ 846 7888 ✉ 477 New North Rd ☺ lunch & dinner 🚇 Kingsland ♿

Fish (6, B2)
Fish & chipper $$
High-backed booths in sexy surrounds (décor and waiters included) with your choice of fish – battered, crumbed or grilled. Your potatoes come chipped, au gratin or (shock, horror) skipped altogether – substituted with rice.
☎ 846 3474 ☐ www.fishcafe.co.nz ✉ 462 New North Rd ☺ lunch Wed-Fri, dinner daily 🚇 Kingsland

Fridge (6, A2)
Deli-café $$
Tables are scarce at this bulging deli, where produce takes priority. Fridge's cakes are worth writing home about.
☎ 845 5321 ✉ 507 New North Rd ☺ brunch/lunch 🚇 Kingsland

Mekong Neua (6, B2)
Thai & Laotian $$
Linen-dressed tables carry superb regional dishes that aren't shy to get spicy. Turn up the heat with the Laos-style country-veg curry or keep it mellow with lemon-scented prawns delicately dabbed with garlic, ginger and chilli.
☎ 846 0323 ✉ 483 New North Rd ☺ dinner 🚇 Kingsland

Entertainment

Auckland is famous for providing the fluff element of culture: crammed with cinemas, music venues, theatres and sporting arenas. Bar options range from savouring an expertly muddled cocktail cross-legged on a velveteen couch to a roughly poured pot of beer in surrounds that are hosed out come cleaning time. The line between clubs and bars is blurry, so don't dismiss dance clubs as all hands-in-the-air hoohaa; some are also good for more melody-inspired moves. Find out what's on by picking up a free copy of *Groove Guide* or the *Fix*, both free weekly guides available in cafés. Friday's *NZ Herald* also has entertainment listings.

BARS & PUBS

Chapel Bar & Bistro (8, B3)
A corner location allows two Ponsonby people-watching aspects; it's a bar *and* bistro; and it has indoor *and* outdoor seating. It's friendly and casual with undeniable appeal.
☎ 360 4528 ⌨ www
.chapel.co.nz ✉ cnr
Ponsonby Rd & Anglesea St,
Ponsonby ⏰ from noon
daily 🚍 Link

Gin Room (2, B2)
This upstairs plush, retro parlour, with dappled chandelier light just touching the many nooks and crannies, may have you reminiscing about the good ole colonial days: when drinking G&Ts was for the quinine in the tonic.
☎ 377 1821 ✉ Level 1,
12 Vulcan Lane, Auckland
⏰ from 5pm Wed-Fri, from
7pm Sat 🚍 Link

Honey (2, B2)
Glide on in to Honey for its accomplished range of beverages from the country's back yard, such as the yummy 42 Below vodka infused with manuka honey or feijoa. The hubbub is usually about the state of the film industry, and who's saying what about whom in the latest glossy.
☎ 369 5639 ✉ 5 O'Connell
St, Auckland ⏰ 4pm-late
🚍 Link

Lenin Bar (2, B1)
The iron curtain has been replaced with a classy glass one, affording twinkling night-time views. March up to Lenin's curvaceous bar and order one of their 80-odd vodkas, including home-infusions, plus potato and grain varieties from around the world. DJs incite dance-floor action Thursday to Saturday.
☎ 377 0040 ✉ Princes
Wharf, 201 Quay St, Auckland ⏰ 3pm-late 🚍 Link

Loaded Hog (2, A1)
People get loaded at the home-style Hog on weekends, but it's a tad tamer during the day and early evening, with

Hee-haw! Get loaded at the Loaded Hog

FESTIVALS & EVENTS

Visitors centres keep a list of most regular events, which are also published online at www.aucklandnz.com/VisitorInformation/Events.

January

Auckland Anniversary Day Regatta (www.regatta.org.nz) A plethora of waterfront and harbour-based activities ought to float your boat.

February

Auckland Festival (www.aucklandfestival.co.nz) International and local music, theatre, visual arts, dance and comedy come together every two years in odd-numbered years.

Devonport Food & Wine Festival (www.devonportwinefestival.co.nz) Dig in.

HERO Festival (www.hero.org.nz) Party hearty with the gay, lesbian, bi and transsexual (GLBT) community at events such as the Big Gay Out and drag-king workshops.

March

Lantern Festival (www.aucklandcity.govt.nz) Albert Park is all aflutter with lanterns on this, the final day of Chinese New Year celebrations. (Sometimes falls in February.)

Pasifika Festival (www.aucklandcity.govt.nz) Western Springs Park hosts this legendary, giant Polynesian party.

Royal NZ Easter Show (www.royaleastershow.co.nz) Agriculturally themed family fun.

Waiheke Jazz Festival (www.waihekejazz.co.nz) The island's popular annual jazz jam.

May

International Comedy Festival (www.comedyfestival.co.nz) Weeks-long laughfest starring local and international comedians.

NZ Boat Show (www.thenewzealandboatshow.co.nz) One of the world's best yachting nations shows off its wares.

June

48hours Furious filmmaking, with shorts made from go to whoa in two days. TV station C4 broadcasts finalists nationally.

August

K Road Fringe Arts Festival If it's left of centre you can revel in it at this multidiscipline (theatre, film, art, dance, music and poetry) arts fest.

October

Aotearoa Hip Hop Summit (www.hiphopnz.com) A celebration of all things hip-hop: graffiti art to MCing and DJing.

Fashion Week (www.nzfashionweek.com) In a city that's full of smart designers, this week is no small treat.

November

Ellerslie Flower Show (www.ellerslieflowershow.co.nz) Five days of flowers, music and food lure crowds to the Auckland Botanic Gardens.

December

Auckland Cup The biggest thoroughbred race of the year, worth a cool $600,000.

Christmas in the Park A party so big it has to be held in the Auckland Domain.

First Night (www.firstnight.org.nz; 31 Dec) A free and alcohol-free party in Aotea Sq and Centre.

Festival revellers get in a tangle

harbourside seating. Home-brews outdo the pretty average pub grub on offer.
☎ 366 6491 ☐ www
.loadedhog.co.nz ✉ 204
Quay St, Viaduct Harbour
☼ 11am-late 🚌 Link

Minus 5° Bar (2, B1)
Known for its extraordinary décor, Minus 5° is carved entirely from ice. Warmth comes with your entry fee by way of fur-lined jackets, gloves and a vodka. And don't get too carried away looking at Victor the ice carver's latest sculptures, you have only half an hour before Jack Frost starts a knockin'.
☎ 377 6702 ☐ www.minus5
.co.nz ✉ Princes Wharf,
Auckland $ adult/child
$25/12 ☼ 2-10pm 🚌 Link

Musket Room (8, C3)
Behind an unassuming door bearing a sign the size of a postage stamp, the Musket Room is easy to miss. But try not to; its owners come from a heritage of hospitality, and its solid stellar reputation is backed by tasty tapas and expertly prepared drinks.
☎ 376 1430 ✉ 29
Ponsonby Rd, Ponsonby
☼ Wed-Sun 🚌 Link

Whiskey (8, B2)
Whiskey gives a nod to the basement bars of New York with its dim, intimate interior. Spot your favourite old-school soft rocker among the black-and-whites lining the walls; one of whom will invariably be providing the soundtrack to that whiskey sour you're sipping.
☎ 361 2666 ✉ 210
Ponsonby Rd, Ponsonby
☼ 5pm-3am 🚌 Link

Watch out for polar bears at Minus 5° Bar

GAY, LESBIAN, BI & TRANSSEXUAL

While the gay and lesbian communities permeate all of Auckland, the scene really comes out to play along K Rd. *Express* is a fortnightly magazine with masses of useful information on the gay and lesbian community. Also check out www.gaynz .com for news and venue listings.

Family (7, B2)
The best gay bar in the city, Family doubles as a club and sets aside certain nights for entertainment offerings. Regulars might do it their way on karaoke night or laugh along with the drag divas.
☎ 309 0213 ✉ 270 K Rd,
Newton ☼ to late daily
🚌 Link

Flesh (2, B2)
A low-lit central bar serves up snacks and karaoke or DJ sounds in loungey surrounds. Downstairs, the club (from 11pm Friday and Saturday)

puts on a drag show that's anything but a drag.
☎ 336 1616 ✉ 17
O'Connell St, Auckland
☼ 6pm-late 🚌 Link

Kamo (7, B2)
While not exclusively gay, Kamo's high-camp Poly-nesian flourishes are…well, gay – in the old sense of the word. Also serving food, Kamo attracts a youngish crowd.
☎ 377 2313 ✉ 382 K
Rd, Newton ☼ 10.30am-10.30pm Tue-Thu, to late Fri & Sat 🚌 Link

Urge (7, A2)
This men-only bar and club has seen a lot of cruising (and a lot of moustaches) in its eight-plus years. Club nights might include Underware, an excuse to get your gear off; or the Steam Room, an excuse to get your gear off. Get the idea? Get your gear off!
☎ 307 2155 ☐ www
.urgebar.co.nz ✉ 490 K Rd,
Newton ☼ 9pm-late Thu-Sat 🚌 Link

DANCE CLUBS

Boogie Wonderland (2, B2)

If you can see the dance floor through the hundreds of pairs of dancin' feet, you'd see its coloured dancing squares. Strictly disco, Boogie is a forgiving kind of place, which may explain the door queues.

☎ 361 6093 ✉ cnr Customs & Queen Sts, Auckland $ $10 cover ⊙ Wed-Sat 🚌 Link

Float (2, B1)

Your basic garden-variety club with each night bringing a different crowd-pleasing flavour. Everything from R & B through to funk. Join gangs of girlfriends and an older crew on their big night out.

☎ 307 1344 🖳 www.float .co.nz ✉ Shed 19, Princes Wharf, Auckland ⊙ Wed-Sat 🚌 Link

Fu Bar (2, B2)

Where the hip-hop doesn't stop. Unless the DJs are doin' drum 'n' bass, or this basement club is hosting local live acts such as Die! Die! Die!

☎ 309 3079 🖳 www .fu.co.nz ✉ 166 Queen St, Auckland $ occasional door charges ⊙ 10pm-late Wed-Sat 🚌 Link

Khuja Lounge (7, C2)

Three floors up in a decadent Art Deco building (warble up in the rickety lift if you dare), Khuja Lounge is a North African–style delight, with name DJs and musicians. Be inspired by the soul, jazz and hip-hop sounds to bump hips on the dance floor or sink 'em into a couch.

☎ 377 3711 🖳 www .khujalounge.co.nz ✉ 536 Queen St, Auckland $ $5-10 ⊙ 8pm-3am Wed-Sat 🚌 Link

Papa Jack's Voodoo Lounge (2, B2)

With a tear just there and a tight skull T-shirt you're all set for Papa Jack's. This rock-and-roll refuge is antichic: where you can carve up the floor with some air-guitar moves or watch (and hear) the real thing on Wednesday.

☎ 358 4847 ✉ 9 Vulcan Lane, Auckland ⊙ 7pm-late Tue-Sat 🚌 Link

CINEMAS

There are no days off for Auckland's hardworking cinemas. Sessions start around 11am, with the last screening at around 9.30pm. Movie prices are generally cheapest on 'tight-arse Tuesday'.

Academy Cinema (2, B3)

Up for a bit of art-house escapism? The boutique Academy screens a steady diet of foreign and independent films that may never have a mainstream cinema release. It's also the venue for the likes of the World Cinema Showcase and Human Rights film festivals.

☎ 373 2761 🖳 www .academy-cinema.co.nz ✉ basement, Central City Library, 44 Lorne St, Auckland $ adult $11-14 🚌 Link

Lido (3, B3)

Auckland's adored cinema, Lido's fat seats in its two licensed theatres make it the people's choice for seeing a flick. Couples should book the back row with removable armrests. Lido screens

---

POLY-WOOD

A couple of recent-release New Zealand films have added to the country's illustrious filmmaking reputation. The difference with these two is their almost entirely Polynesian casts – something that wouldn't have been possible 10 years ago; there just wasn't the audience. *No 2* is the film adaptation of the same-name stage play that brought bums to every seat during its national tour. It's an art-house feast that screened at the venerable Sundance film festival in 2006. The film centres on a matriarch's feast, at which she'll name her successor. By contrast, the populist *Sione's Wedding* follows four fellows looking for suitable ladies to take to a family wedding. It's been likened to a chick flick for blokes, and features the clubs and bars of K Rd and Ponsonby. While neither film is an all-pervading truth of NZ's Islander population (one in seven people), the films' very existence gives the Pacific Islander community a lively and confident voice.

art house, foreign and the odd Hollywood film.

☎ 630 1500 💻 www.lido cinema.co.nz ✉ 427 Manukau Rd, Epsom 💲 adult $10-14 🚍 Link

NZ Film Archives (7, B2)

This fabulous film resource has over a thousand Kiwi feature films and documentaries (dating from 1905) that you can view on a large telly. Perhaps the beautifully rendered tale of a family's '70s summer in *Rain*. Or the never-a-dry-eye Maori tale of *Whale Rider*, or a Jackson classic such as *Heavenly Creatures*.

☎ 379 0688 💻 www .filmarchive.org.nz ✉ 300 K Rd, Newton 🕑 11am-5pm Mon-Fri, to 4pm Sat 🚍 Link

Rialto Cinemas (3, B3)

Drama, horror, comedy and kids' movies. This large independent chain has cinemas across the country. Licensed.

☎ 529 2218 💻 www .rialto.co.nz ✉ 167 Broadway, Newmarket 💲 $8.50-15 🚍 Link

Village Sky City Megascreen (2, B3)

Watch the latest mainstream movie in a frenzy of popcorn and ice-cream consumption. Part of the modernistic Metro mall, slipping into a darkened cinema makes for a great escape from the crude fluoro flood. Go for Gold Class ($25-35) where the popcorn is replaced with butter-chicken skewers and the waitstaff keeps your flute topped with champers.

☎ 979 2401 💻 www .villageskycity.co.nz ✉ Level 3, 291 Queen St, Auckland 💲 $8.50-15 🚍 Link

LIVE MUSIC

Dogs Bollix (7, A3)

This little Irish pub has a big reputation, putting on something to entertain the punters every night. If it's not a band belting out original numbers, it's a trivia night or big-TV sports telecast.

☎ 376 4600 💻 www.dogs bollixirishbar.co.nz ✉ cnr K & Newton Rds, Newton 💲 free-$10 🕑 4pm-late Mon-Wed, 11.30am-late Thur-Sun 🚍 Link

Eden's Bar (7, A3)

This sweaty space is always in what's-on lists. And to prove how many bands play here, the front is plastered with posters. Expect wall-of-noise guitar-based rock.

✉ 335 K Rd, Newton 💲 varies 🕑 Wed-Sun

Galatos (7, B2)

A converted theatre, Galatos hosts bands in the basement and DJs and club nights in the main room, the parquet floor of which has seen the gamut

BOOKING TICKETS

Tickets for major sport events, plus theatre and concerts, are often available directly from the venue's box office. If not, one of the following agencies take credit-card bookings.

Ticketek (☎ 307 5000; http://premier.ticketek .co.nz)

TicketMaster (☎ 970 9700; www.ticketmaster .co.nz)

Have a drink with the wee green people at the Dogs Bollix

Expect high drama at Aotea Centre

of dance styles from the cha-cha in its ballroom days to current hands-in-the-air DJ worship. The upstairs Lounge is home to the **Moving Image Centre** (www.mic.org.nz), which screens new-media.

☎ 303 1928 ▢ www.galatos.co.nz ✉ 17 Galatos St, Newton $ free-$15 ☽ 9pm-late Wed-Sun

Kings Arms Tavern (7, B3)
A rite of passage to get into the local scene, the King's Arms is one of the city's leading small venues. This old reliable has a great garden bar. Fancy it ain't, so you could even luck in on a game of darts or sport on the telly.

☎ 373 3240 ▢ www.kingsarms.co.nz ✉ 59 France St, Newton $ free-$5 ☽ 11am-late ▣ Link

Rakinos (2, B3)
A mild-mannered café and bar the rest of the week, come Thursday Rakinos cranks with DJs and bands. It covers a lot of bases, so makes a fitting finish or start to any night.

☎ 358 3535 ✉ 35 High St, Auckland $ free-$10 ☽ Thu-Sat

THEATRE, CLASSICAL & COMEDY

Classic Comedy Club (7, C1)
Built for laughs, the Classic has proven to be the city's top comedy venue. See local comedians and comediennes stand up (and sometimes fall) during the venue's regular performance programme.

☎ 373 4321 ▢ www.comedy.co.nz ✉ 321 Queen St, Auckland $ $5-15 ▣ Link

Edge
A quartet of performing-arts venues comes under the Edge's collective management. They're all within a ticket's toss of one another, and each favours a specific style. They include Aotea Square (see p27) and the imposing **Auckland Town Hall** (4, B4; ☎ 309 2677; 50 Mayoral Dr), its Great Hall often filled with the sounds of residents: the Symphony Orchestra (www.aucklandsymphony.gen.nz) and Philharmonia (www.aucklandphil.co.nz). The **Aotea Centre** (4, B4; ☎ 307 5060; 50 Mayoral Dr) is the main venue for the classics: expect high drama from the Auckland Theatre Company (www.atc.co.nz), the NZ Opera company (www.nzopera.com) and the Royal New Zealand Ballet (www.nzballet.or.nz). Not least is the grand dame of theatre, the **Civic** (2, B3; ☎ 309 2677; www.civic

BIG-TICKET VENUES

- **Bruce Mason Centre** (3, A1; ☎ 488 2940; www.bmcentre.co.nz; cnr Hurstmere Rd & the Promenade, Takapuna) North Shore's busiest venue, hosting citizens' ceremonies, competitions (like the NZ Body Art Awards) and concerts – might be an orchestra, might be Cliff Richard.
- **Eden Park** (3, A3; ☎ 815 5551; www.edenpark.co.nz) It's *the* stadium for top rugby (winter) and cricket (summer) matches. The All Blacks, the Black Caps and the Auckland Blues all play here.
- **Ericsson Stadium** (3, B4; ☎ 571 6303; www.ericssonstadium.co.nz; Beasley Ave, Penrose) Mostly rugby league.
- **North Shore Events Centre** (3, A1; ☎ 849 3807; www.nseventscentre.co.nz; Porana Rd, Glenfield) Netball and basketball, plus exhibition-style events.
- **Western Springs Stadium** (3, A3; ☎ 849 3807; Western Springs) This megavenue, centred on a natural amphitheatre, recently hosted the Stones. Robbie Williams, U2 and Bowie have also played here, plus it's a regular speedway venue – very unpopular with local residents.

theatre.co.nz; cnr Queen & Wellesley Sts). Its starry ceiling has seen cinema, theatre and opera since opening in 1929.

☎ 309 2677 🖳 www.the-edge.co.nz ✉ Queen St, Auckland 🚍 Link

Silo Theatre (7, C1)
With an annual programme that presents current plays, past plays, locally devised theatre and overseas theatre, it's not easy to pin down the Silo. Past plays have included Toa Fraser's *No 2*, plus those from playwrights of the ilk of Neil La Bute (US), Dylan Thomas (Wales) and Louis Nowra (Australia).

☎ 366 0339 🖳 www.silo theatre.co.nz ✉ Lower Greys Ave, Auckland 💲 $17-35 🚍 Link

SPORTS

Sailing

The 'City of Sails' has almost 50 sailing and boating clubs. It has also left an indelible stamp on the international competitions circuit since winning the holy grail of yachting, the America's Cup, in 1995 and hosting the challenge in 2003 centred on Viaduct Harbour

(p9). Team NZ lost the duel to landlocked Switzerland (whose boat was skippered and partly crewed by New Zealanders). Look out for other major competitions with the Royal New Zealand Yacht Squadron (www .rnzys.org.nz), usually between January and April. Or get on board and sail yourself (p17).

Rugby

Rugby Union's national team is the All Blacks. One rung below this top international level sits the Super 14 competition (with teams from Australia and South Africa), then there's the National Provincial Championship.

Auckland is home to the NZ Warriors rugby league team, which plays in the Australian National Rugby League (NRL). Supporting the Warriors has become a way into the culture for South Auckland immigrant communities, and a Warriors home game at Ericsson Stadium is a noisy spectacle.

Cricket

Friends and family turn up to Eden Park to support the district cricket (www.aucklandcricket.co.nz), while the world watches the Black Caps play internationally in the Test matches and World Series Cup one-day matches. Check out www.nzcricket.co.nz for schedules and information.

Tennis

The ladies thwock it to 'em during the ASB Classic, while famous tennis chaps serve up at the Heineken Tennis Open. Both are held in January at the ASB Bank Tennis Centre (4, D4; ☎ 373 3623; www.aucklandtennis .co.nz; 1 Tennis Lane, Parnell).

Sleeping

Across Auckland you can find some shuteye in a range of surrounds: from bare bones to spare nothing.

B&B accommodation in private homes may be in mansions or humble cottages. The comprehensive *B&B Directory of New Zealand* (www.bed-and-breakfast.co.nz) is available online, at bookshops and from visitors centres. The city has plenty of hotels, including five-star internationals, boutique places and mid-range options, all of which charge according to their level of facilities. Most motels are drive-up, modernish places, with basic facilities and '70s décor. In the budget category, New Zealand is the place that pioneered the term 'flashpacker', with spiffy purpose-built hostel-style accommodation that cares about cleanliness and offers the gamut of shared facilities. Parking prices range from free to $20 a day; check when making your booking.

ROOM RATES

The categories indicate the cost per night of a standard double room in high season.

Top End	over $201
Midrange	$101-200
Budget	under $100

Très elegant décor at Quest Ponsonby

Peak tourist seasons (when accommodation is in high demand and at its priciest) include from Christmas to the end of January and Easter. At other times, you might find weekend rates cheaper at business-style hotels. And walk-in rates are sometimes available towards the end of the day.

The NZ visitors centre (p58) has accommodation listings and can make bookings. Booking online often bags the best deals. For more accommodation reviews written by Lonely Planet authors see Haystack, the online booking service at www.lonelyplanet.com. Travellers should also check websites such as www.wotif.com for last-minute discounts.

TOP END

Esplanade Hotel (5, A3)
High-ceilinged rooms allow space for more luxury than at most hotels. The venerable curvilinear Edwardian building basks in its waterfront position; its 15 rooms furnished in period fashion.
☎ 445 1291 ☐ www.esplanadehotel.co.nz ✉ 1 Victoria Rd, Devonport ☐ Devonport ☐ ✗ Esplanade Restaurant (p35) & bar on site ♿

Great Ponsonby B&B (8, A2)
Wake up cheery, ensconced in your big bed surrounded by warm colours, designer flourishes and with a homemade breakfast ready when you are. This spacious 11-room villa is a short stride away from bustling Ponsonby Rd.
☎ 376 5989 ☐ www.greatpons.co.nz ✉ 30 Ponsonby Tce, Ponsonby ☐ airport shuttle ✗ p34

Hilton Hotel (2, A1)
The city's swankiest big-name hotel perches at the tip of Princes Wharf – resembling a luxury oceanliner in both scale and sumptuousness. Super service, big bathrooms and classy facilities might have you bursting onto your balcony proclaiming you're the 'King of the World'.
☎ 978 2000 ☐ www.hilton.co.nz ✉ Princes Wharf, Auckland ☐ airport shuttle ☐ ✗ ☐ ✗ White (p32) on site ♿

Scenic Circle Airedale Hotel (7, C1)

This delightful Art Deco building's loving makeover has seen it transformed from office tower to tower of chic sleep. Business types still flock here during the week, but not to work – rather to flop on the big bed after a home-cooked meal prepared in the cosy kitchenette.
☎ 374 1741 ☐ www.scenic-circle.co.nz ✉ 380 Queen St, Auckland 🚌 airport shuttle Ⓟ ✄ 🖥 ✖ MLC café & bar on site ♿

Sebel Suites (2, A1)

High-finish, super-stylish suites, with smooth service and top-end details prop high above glistening Viaduct Harbour. These open-plan studio-style apartments provide a very cushy landing after a hard day's sightseeing.
☎ 978 4000 ☐ www.mirvachotels.com.au ✉ 85 Customs St West, Auckland 🚌 airport shuttle Ⓟ ✖ p32 ♿

Sky City Grand Hotel (2, A3)

Lap up the luxury in the lap pool, gymnasium and health spa before retiring to your stunning five-star room. There's little more you'll want for here, with some services you may wish you didn't request – that's your personal trainer knocking.
☎ 363 6000 ☐ www.skycity.co.nz ✉ cnr Victoria & Federal Sts, Auckland 🚌 airport shuttle Ⓟ ✄ 🖥 ✖ restaurants & cocktail lounge on site ♿ babysitting service

Do a few leisurely laps in the Hilton's oceanliner-style pool

MIDRANGE

Abaco Spa Motel (8, B1)

This handsome, neutral-toned motel in the Ponsonby throng is big on homely comforts. Pad from the stainless-steel kitchenette to the spa while wrapped in a fluffy white towel, then put your pruned self into the big bed.
☎ 360 6850 ☐ www.abaco.co.nz ✉ 59 Jervois Rd, Ponsonby 🚌 airport shuttle Ⓟ ✄ 🖥 ✖ p34 ♿

Braemer on Parliament (4, D3)

This precious historic house has played host to many a notable New Zealander and weary traveller for decades. Exquisite restorations mean quality lion-foot tub time for guests.
☎ 377 5463 ☐ www.aucklandbedandbreakfast.com ✉ 7 Parliament St, Auckland 🚌 airport shuttle ✖ p31

Freeman's B&B (4, A4)

All those flash accoutrements at other hotels are no good to you when you're asleep. So say Freeman's fans who appreciate the good-value solid standards here. Go for the B&B option or the two-bedroom apartment.
☎ 376 5046 ☐ www.freemansbandb.co.nz ✉ 65 Wellington St, Ponsonby 🚌 airport shuttle ✖ p34 ♿

Fringe of Heaven (1, B2)

The guest bedroom in this stylish '50s-inspired home has you waking in the trees, with just a glass panel between you and them. This city escape gives you your own cushy loungeroom, and sea or city views from every room in the house are truly inspiring.
☎ 817 8682 ☐ www.fringeofheaven.com ✉ 4 Otitori Rd, Titirangi 🚌 30 mins southwest of central Auckland Ⓟ

Heritage Auckland (2, A2)

High-class features distinguish this national chain hotel. Traditionalists should choose the hotel's heritage wing, while businessfolk should beeline for the newer Tower. Everyone: run to the rooftop pool.
☎ 379 8553 ☐ www.heritagehotels.co.nz ✉ 35 Hobson St, Auckland 🚌 airport shuttle Ⓟ ✄ 🖥 ✖ restaurant & bar on site ♿ babysitting service

Herne Bay B&B (8, A1)

Delivering stlye and substance, rooms here are lush and large. There is a range of configurations – choose an en suite or shared-facility room.
☎ 360 0309 ☐ www.herne-bay.co.nz ✉ 4 Shelly Beach Rd, Herne Bay 🚌 airport shuttle Ⓟ ✖ p34

BEACH OR BUSH BACH

The basic Kiwi holiday home is called a 'bach', short for 'bachelor' (and pronounced 'batch'), as they were often used by single men as hunting and fishing retreats. These often-simple, self-contained cottages can be rented in Auckland's bays, beaches and bushland. Check out www.bookabach.co.nz for options.

Parnell Inn (4, E5)

Rooms at the Inn meld sentimental touches (pillow chocolates) with newer features like posh-looking silk bedspreads. Being perched in hilly Parnell provides fab harbour views from some rooms too.
☎ 358 0642 🖳 www.parnell inn.co.nz ✉ 320 Parnell Rd, Parnell 🚌 airport shuttle 🅿 🖳 ✖ p34 ♿

Quest Ponsonby (8, C3)

Handsome self-contained apartments are perfectly located among the cafés, restaurants and boutiques of Ponsonby Rd. Enormous comfy beds, bathrooms with washing machine and dryer, plus a kitchenette (fridge and microwave) bring homely conveniences to any holiday

or business trip. Machinery noise from the yeast factory abutting the back of the building may get a rise from guests staying in the back rooms.
☎ 360 4240 🖳 www .questapartments.com .au ✉ 68 Ponsonby Rd, Ponsonby 🅿 ✖ ✖ p34

Rainbow Hotel (2, A3)

At the bottom of the Rainbow are weeny rooms at budget prices. The higher up you go, the more those walls expand – right up to self-contained family apartments. The shared kitchen is a bonus for budgeteers.
☎ 356 7272 🖳 www.rain bowhotel.co.nz ✉ cnr Nelson & Wellesley Sts, Auckland 🚌 airport shuttle 🅿 ✖ 🖳 ✖ p31 ♿

BUDGET

Aspen House (2, C2)

Smart, simple and affordable, this super option is the nexus between hotel and B&B: where you get a basic breakfast without having to speak to anyone before the caffeine kicks in. It's located on a steep central street, a few blocks from precious Albert Park.
☎ 379 6633 🖳 www.aspen house.co.nz ✉ 62 Emily Pl, Auckland 🚌 airport shuttle 🅿 🖳 ✖ p31 ♿

City Garden Lodge (4, E5)

Originally built for the Queen of Tonga, this two-storey timber house is now a friendly, well-run backpackers. Hang on the balcony in a hammock, or do the yoga class on the front lawn.
☎ 302 0880 🖳 www.city gardenlodge.co.nz ✉ 25 St Georges Bay Rd, Parnell 🚌 airport shuttle 🖳 ✖ p34

City Lodge (7, B1)

Slick, shiny and central, City Lodge is a great budget bet. All rooms come with stamp-sized bathrooms and access to the equipped industrial kitchen and comfy TV room.
☎ 379 6183 🖳 www.city lodge.co.nz ✉ 150 Vincent St, Auckland ✖ p31

Surf & Snow (2, B3)

A backpackers with top-notch credo for cleanliness. Good facilities (including laundry, kitchen and kiosk) and bright multilingual staff make this central place great value.
☎ 363 8889 🖳 www.surf andsnow.co.nz ✉ 102 Albert St, Auckland 🚌 airport shuttle 🖳 ✖ p31

HISTORY
Once Upon a Time

In darkness, Tane-mahuta (God of the Forests, represented by the kauri tree) placed his shoulders down against his mother, Papatuanuku (Earth Mother), and used his feet to push up against his father, Ranginui (Sky Father) – separating the two, and letting in light. New Zealand's first settlers, the Maori, imbued the land with significant spiritual and cultural meaning. As competition for resources increased, so too did intertribal conflict, which led to Maori building sophisticated fortifications, known as *pa*, the vestiges of which are still visible on hill tops across Auckland.

Colonial Conquests & Conflicts

European contact has been recorded as early as 1642, with numerous subsequent explorations motivated by science, profit and power. Northland saw the majority of early contact. Some interracial violence ensued, though it was relatively modest. Maori benefited from the European's pigs and potatoes, though suffered from their diseases and muskets. Weapons devastated the Maori population during intertribal conflicts known as the Musket Wars (1813–36), with the loss of an estimated 20,000 Maori lives.

NZ became a British colony in 1840 with the contested Treaty of Waitangi. The original problem was a discrepancy between Maori and British understandings of it. The English version omitted Maori's rights to local government. Conflict brewed.

In 1841 NZ's first governor, William Hobson, proclaimed Auckland as capital, but in 1865 the seat of government was moved from Auckland to Wellington – in the middle of the government-assisted mass immigration of the 1850s and 1870s. The influx of European settlers and the increasing demand for land sparked the Land Wars, a series of conflicts between Pakeha (European New Zealanders) and Maori, motivated by land rights.

A *marae* (the sacred ground in front of a Maori meeting house)

A Kind of Capital

Despite conflict with Maoris, the Pakeha economy boomed. The city's ports and international airport are the conduits for the country's exports, constituting the lion's share of the nation's economic activity. Auckland continues to be built on and refreshed by migration, as well as by an increase in its Maori population.

Since the beginning of the 20th century, Auckland has been NZ's fastest growing city and its main industrial centre.

THE AUTHOR OF AUCKLAND

He gave an evocative account of early Auckland in his book *Poenamo*. But more so, John Logan Campbell (1871–1912) gave Auckland: Cornwall Park (p18), a brewery (that grew to become Lion Nathan), an arts school (that became Elam, the city's premier fine-arts institution), and the impetus to establish the University of Auckland. Oh, and he represented Auckland as a minister and a mayor. There's little doubt that Campbell's hand guided the story of this city.

ENVIRONMENT

Environmentalism is a national pastime – the majority of New Zealanders hyper-aware of their responsibility to protect their gorgeous environment.

Aucklanders are avid recyclers, with councils committed to reducing waste for landfill to zero. The city's ever-expanding population is expected to double by 2050, placing enormous pressure on resources. Pre-emptive government planning aims to curb urban sprawl and limit the impact on the region's country areas. Auckland's air pollution levels exceed those of London – thanks to the region's 650,000 cars, responsible for 80% of the city's overall emissions. On the bright side, the city's water quality is excellent, with drinking water among the world's best.

Famously, Greenpeace's *Rainbow Warrior* was sank in Auckland Harbour in 1985 by the French Security Forces to thwart the environmental organisation's planned antinuclear campaign in French territory.

GOVERNMENT & POLITICS

Auckland is administered by four separate city councils, each with its own mayor: Auckland City, North Shore, Waitakere and Manukau. City councils govern on a local level (concerned with the supply of essential services), and work with the country's central government. Central government supports city initiatives deemed beneficial to the overall country.

Aucklanders are politically aware, which naturally follows from denizens of the biggest city in a politically progressive nation. NZ was the

DID YOU KNOW?

- Auckland's average weekly wage is among the country's highest (at over $800 gross)
- The lowest level of satisfaction with work-life balance was recorded in Auckland
- The average house price in Auckland is around $475,000
- About 13 million people visit Auckland each year, worth over $3 billion to the economy

first country in the world to give women the vote (1893), and is currently under the prime ministership of Helen Clark. And it's a country renowned for its government's antinuclear stance, and responsible social policies.

ECONOMY

Auckland is key in the country's prosperous economy. Though the nation's economy is founded on the sheep's back, Auckland sustains the country's trade, business and finance sector. It's NZ's largest centre for employment, and the region's hub of professional services, cultural activity and higher education. The city's ports (both shipping and air) see three-quarters of the country's imports and 40% of its exports. Auckland dominates traveller arrivals, and is HQ for NZ's mass media. Tourism is one of the country's largest export industries. This all augers well for the visitor: Auckland being a lively city presenting a range of recreational activities buoyed by its economic- and cultural-centre status.

SOCIETY & CULTURE

Designer clobber and a shiny 4WD car: Aucklanders are perceived as brash, nouveau riche and shallow by noncity-dwelling New Zealanders, who even have a name for them: JAFA (Just Another Fucking Auck-lander). Aucklanders, on the other hand, see themselves as nature-loving folk who work hard (40% of them in the property-and-business sector) to expand the country in areas other than agriculture, such as tertiary education, business services and creative industries.

Auckland *is* unique from the rest of the country. It's the world's largest Polynesian city: home to more Pacific Islanders than the Pacific Islands themselves. It has a significant and growing Maori population as well as Asian immigrants, such that almost one in three Aucklanders identify themselves as either Maori, Pacific Islander or Asian. New Zealanders from other parts of the country contribute large numbers to the city's burgeoning population too: coining the term 'northern drift'.

In the main, Aucklanders are not considered a particularly pious population. Deemed more likely to find spiritual fulfilment outdoors than in a formal place of worship.

Etiquette

Auckland is literally a polite society, which demonstrates good manners. Aucklanders will help if they can, so don't be shy to ask anyone for directions. Smoking is banished to the pavement: don't light up in bars or restaurants. And business conduct is straightforward: astute candour seals the deal.

A Polynesian dancer struts his stuff

ARTS

Auckland's arts are socially in-valuable, and increasingly ac-knowledged for their significant economic contribution. The city's critical mass of creative talent manifests in myriad easily acces-sible ways.

Literature

Auckland's North Shore has a dis-proportionately high number of accomplished authors and publish-ers. It's been a literary hub since the 1930s, when authors explored the Kiwi identity as independent from the dominant British one

Aaron Kereopa with his carved surfboard

adopted virtually by proxy. For most, there's a distinct relationship with nature, such as in the polemic poems of ARD Fairburn and Kevin Ireland. Novelists dealing with the complexities of city life include Noel Virtue and Chad Taylor.

Music

Song, dance, rhythm and melody are woven tightly into Maori culture, and it's never been stronger or more varied. Maori and Pacific Island artists increasingly bounce out of the airwaves, which play about 20% NZ music. K Rd's clubs feature the city's top DJs and MCs, like Mareko and Savage.

Auckland is home to the garage-rock scene that provided a springboard for the D4 and the Datsuns; catch would-bes at the Kings Arms (p42).

Visual Arts

In a nation defined by its natural environment, it's not surprising that early Pakeha painting was defined by the landscape genre. Portraiture fol-lowed. Most notably, Charles Goldie's detailed representations of Maoris – perceived as a dying race.

Subsequently, visual arts has expanded to incorporate photography, sculpture and technology. The Auckland Museum (p8) has an extraordin-ary collection of traditional Maori and Pacific artefacts. The Auckland Art Gallery (p13) displays Goldie's work, while boutique contemporary galleries are found across town (see p16).

TITILLATING TITIRANGI

Nestled in the Waitakere Ranges, 13km southwest of downtown Auckland, Titirangi (www.titirangi.net) is renowned for its stunning surrounds and arty inhabitants, includ-ing musician Neil Finn and, previously, photographer Brian Brake and painter Colin Mc-Cahon. Main street's **Lopdell House** (☎ 817 8087; www.lopdell.org.nz; 418 Titirangi Rd; ☽ 10am-4.30pm) is the region's premier exhibition space for contemporary art and theatre.

Directory

ARRIVAL & DEPARTURE
Air
Auckland International Airport (3, B6) is 20km south of downtown Auckland. A free shuttle runs between the airport's domestic and international terminals from 6am to 10.30pm.

INFORMATION
For general inquiries, flight and car-parking information, call ☎ 0800 247 767 or ☎ 275 0789, or visit www.auckland-airport.co.nz. For lost and found, call ☎ 275 0789.

AIRPORT ACCESS
Bus
Airbus (☎ 0508 27 287; www.airbus.co.nz; adult/child $15/6; 1 hour; every 20-30 min) Stops at major accommodation spots downtown, as well as Britomart Transport Centre. The first service from downtown to the airport is at 3.50am (4.35am weekends); the last service is at 8.50pm. Services from the airport start at 4.40am (6am weekends) and finish at 10pm.
Super Shuttle (☎ 0800 748 885, 522 5100; www.supershuttle.co.nz; adult $23; 1 hour; on demand) Door-to-door service that operates 24 hours.

Taxi
A taxi fare between the airport and downtown Auckland costs between $50 and $65. The ride takes a minimum of 30 minutes.

Bus
InterCity Coachlines (☎ 623 1503; www.intercitycoach.co.nz) is the dominant long-distance bus company, connecting most destinations in New Zealand. Intercity Passes can be a cheap and flexible way to get around, covering various popular routes and departing daily. Passes are valid for 12 months so you can jump-on and jump-off at numerous designated points; bookings for each onward section are required two hours in advance. It has four pick-up points in Auckland.

CLIMATE CHANGE & TRAVEL
Travel – especially air travel – is a significant contributor to global climate change. At Lonely Planet, we believe that all travellers have a responsibility to limit their personal impact. As a result, we have teamed with Rough Guides and other concerned industry partners to support Climatecare.org, which allows travellers to offset the greenhouse gases they are responsible for with contributions to sustainable travel schemes. Lonely Planet offsets all staff and author travel. For more information, check out www.lonely planet.com.

Travel Documents
PASSPORT
Passports are required for overseas visitors and must be valid for at least three months beyond the date of departure.

VISA
The **New Zealand Immigration Service** (NZIS; ☎ 0508 558 855, 914 4100; www.immigration.govt.nz) website lists the 50-odd countries from which citizens do not require visas to visit New Zealand. These include Australia, the UK, Canada, France, Germany, Japan, Ireland, the Netherlands and the USA.

Customs & Duty-Free
New Zealand Customs (www.customs.govt.nz) has a duty-free quota per person of 1125mL of spirits or liqueur, 4.5L of wine or beer, 200 cigarettes (or 50 cigars or 250g of tobacco) and dutiable goods up to the value of $700.

Customs people are obviously fussy about illicit drugs and biosecurity, with authorities serious about keeping out any diseases that may harm the country's significant agricultural industry. You must declare any plant or animal products (including anything made of wood), and food of any kind. You'll also come in for extra scrutiny if you've arrived via Africa, Southeast Asia or South America. Weapons and firearms are either prohibited or require a permit and safety testing.

Departure Tax
There is a $25 departure tax. Pay at airport counters before going through customs.

Left Luggage
Wherever you've stayed will generally store your luggage if necessary. Bag storage is also available at the visitor information centre, located on the ground floor of the airport's domestic transfer area; overnight storage rates for a suitcase range from $5 to $10. Storage lockers are also located at Britomart's Travel Centre (☎ 270 5211), within the Transport Centre, on the concourse level; small lockers cost $10 a day and big lockers cost $15 a day. Bags can be stored for up to three days.

GETTING AROUND
Maxx (☎ 366 6400; www.maxx.co.nz) unites Auckland's bus, ferry and train public transport, which are generally reliable and good value. Timetables and fares are listed on the website. The city's transport hub is the **Britomart Transport Centre** (2, B1; www.artnl.co.nz; Queen Elizabeth Sq, Auckland).

In this book, the most convenient transport option is indicated with the appropriate symbol: bus (🚌), ferry (⛴) or train (🚆). Unless otherwise stated, all services depart from Britomart and the Downtown Ferry Building.

Travel Passes
The **Auckland Discovery Day Pass** ($13) allows all-day travel on the city's buses, trains and ferries (excluding travel to islands in the Hauraki Gulf). The **7-Day Pass** ($38) allows unlimited travel on buses, ferries (as far as Devonport) and trains for the week. Both passes are available for purchase from bus drivers, train staff and from the Downtown Ferry Building.

Bus
Auckland's extensive bus network is tabled in the free (and handy) *Busabout Guide,* available from visitors centres and Britomart. Purchase tickets from the driver.

The **Link Bus** ($1.50) is most useful for travel around town. It concurrently loops clockwise and anticlockwise, with departures every 10 to 15 minutes between 6am and 11.30pm Monday to Friday and from 7am to 6pm at weekends; stops include Parnell, K Rd, Ponsonby and the Domain. The free **Circuit** bus links key inner-city destinations, such as the Ferry Building, Sky Tower and Albert Park. It runs every 10 minutes between 8am and 6pm.

Ferry
Fullers (☎ 367 9111; www.fullers.co.nz) operates frequent daily passenger ferries from the Downtown Ferry Building to Devonport on the North Shore and to the Hauraki Gulf islands.

Train
Three train routes run from Britomart: one runs west to Waitakere, and two run south to Pukekohe. Times vary, but they operate roughly between 6am and 9pm.

Taxi
Flagfall is $2 and then $1.75 to $2.10 per kilometre. There's a $4 toll for transport to/from the airport.

Taxis generally cruise popular areas, as well as work from ranks such as on the K Rd bridge (7, A2), the Viaduct (2, B1) and at Federal St (2, A3). Many of the city's taxi companies accept credit cards and take phone bookings.
Alert (☎ 309 4000)
Coop (☎ 300 3000)

Car & Motorcycle
On a short trip to the city you're unlikely to need your own wheels, as inner-city hubs are within 30 minutes' walk of downtown and well connected by public transport.

A car would be handy to get out to and around Waitakere on your own steam, or over on Waiheke.

Some possible car-rental companies include:

A2B (☎ 0800 616 333, 377 0824; www.a2b-car-rental.co.nz)

Europcar (☎ 0800 800 115, 379 5080; www.europcar.co.nz)

Thrifty (☎ 0800 737 070, 03-359 2723; www.thrifty.co.nz)

PRACTICALITIES
Climate & When to Go

Auckland's seaside location makes for some fickle weather: four seasons in one day. The official high season is between the summer months of November and April, particularly during the mid-December to mid-January school-holiday break. Around this time the city hosts numerous festivals and events.

The less-touristy months, either side of the official high season, are the best times to visit: the weather's pleasant, key sights are quieter and you won't have to pay a premium for the privilege.

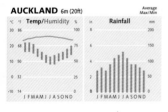

Consulates

Most foreign embassies are based in Wellington, but some countries have consular representation in Auckland; refer to the *Yellow Pages* for a full list.

Australia (2, B1; ☎ 921 8800; www.australia.org.nz; level 7, Price Waterhouse Coopers Bldg, 186-194 Quay St, Auckland)

Canada (2, C2; ☎ 309 3690; www.auckland.gc.ca; level 9, 48 Emily Pl, Auckland)

UK (2, B2; ☎ 303 2973; www.uktradeinvest.co.nz; 151 Queen St, Auckland)

USA (2, C2; ☎ 303 2724; http://newzealand.usembassy.gov; level 3, Citibank Centre, 23 Customs St East, Auckland)

Disabled Travellers

Most of Auckland's key sights, public phones and ATMs are wheelchair accessible. Download (www.aucklandcity.govt.nz/council/projects/disability/map.asp) or phone (☎ 379 2020) for a copy of the council's *Access Auckland Map,* which indicates parking and public toilets, as well as street gradients and other useful information. Most of the city's pedestrian crossings have sight and sound cues.

Further information is available from **Weka** (☎ 0800 171 981; www.weka.net.nz) and the **Disability Resource Centre** (☎ 625 8069; drc@disabilityresource.org.nz).

Discounts

Many of Auckland's attractions offer discounts for children (usually aged between five and 15), families (including between three and six people) and full-time students and seniors (they must show ID). Only Auckland residents are eligible for seniors discounts on public transport, though overseas students with **International Student Travel Confederation** (ISTC; www.istc.org) cards can obtain concession fares. Hostel organisations, such as **BBH** (www.bbh.co.nz) and **YHA** (www.stayyha.com), issue membership cards entitling the user to discounts on accommodation and travel with participating companies.

Electricity

Cycle AC
Frequency 50Hz
Plugs Flat three-pin
Voltage 230V

Emergencies

Auckland isn't a dangerous city, but use big-city common sense; ie avoid a lone boozy walk home through the park late at night.

Ambulance, fire service & police (☎ 111)

Auckland Central Police Station (4, B4; ☎ 302 6400; cnr Vincent & Cook Sts)

Rape Crisis (☎ 360 4004)

Fitness

Auckland is a great city in which to walk. If trudging between suburbs isn't exercise enough, try one of the following activities. See p17 for sailing, kayaking and skating opportunities.

CYCLING

Auckland is a cycling-savvy city, with picturesque paths and challenging hills. Cycling maps indicating popular routes and designated cycle lanes can be downloaded at www.maxx.co.nz/cycle.html. Bikes are allowed on trains ($1), preferably outside peak times, and on Fullers ferries (for free). Helmets are compulsory, as are lights for riding at night.

Hire bikes from Adventure Cycles (p17) or from the **Harbour Info Centre** (2, B1; Ferry Bldg, 99 Quay St; per day $25).

GYMS

Increase your muscle mass by participating in Auckland's significant gym culture. **Les Mills World of Fitness** (4, B3; ☎ 379 9550; www.lesmills.co.nz; 186 Victoria St West, Auckland; casual visit $17.50; ☺ 5.30am-10pm Mon-Thu, 5.30am-9pm Fri, 7am-7pm Sat & Sun) was founded in the late '60s by the city's former mayor. It has a women's-only area, plus yoga sessions.

Some swimming complexes also have gyms; see right.

JOGGING

Keeping fit can be as easy as a pair of sneakers and some loose-fitting shorts. The expanse of green and fringing bushland of Auckland's Domain (p18) makes it a popular running venue. The waterfront, particularly along the flat harbourside Tamaki Dr (east of downtown), also makes for a good run.

SWIMMING

Apart from swimming at beaches along the east coast and North Shore (see boxed text, p17), there are a number of centrally located pools.

Olympic Swimming Pool (4, E6; ☎ 522 4414; 77 Broadway, Newmarket; adult/child/student $6.50/4/5.50; ☺ 5.45am-10pm Mon-Fri, 7am-8pm Sat & Sun) Apart from the 50m pool, there's a spa, steam room, crèche (☎ 522 1532) and gym ($20).

Parnell Baths (4, F3; ☎ 373 3561; Judges Bay Rd; adult/child $5/3; ☺ 6am-8pm Mon-Fri, 8am-8pm Sat & Sun Nov-Apr) Outdoor 60m saltwater pools.

Tepid Baths (2, A1; ☎ 379 4754; 100 Customs St; adult/child $5.50/3; ☺ 6am-9pm Mon-Fri, 7am-7pm Sat & Sun) Has two pools (25m and 18m), a sauna, spa and steam room and a fitness centre ($16.50).

Gay & Lesbian Travellers

The biggest city in a country that legally recognises same-sex unions, Auckland's gay-and-lesbian scene is a visible and valued component of the community. The clubs, cabaret and cafés along K Rd form the focus of the gay, lesbian and transgender scene; see p39 for details.

The **Auckland Pride Centre** (☎ 302 0590; www.pride.org.nz) can advise on upcoming events and preferred community and business services.

Health

IMMUNISATIONS

NZ has no vaccination requirements for any traveller.

PRECAUTIONS

NZ has one of the world's highest rates of skin cancer; wear sunscreen and a hat in summer. The surf north and west of the city poses another summer hazard. Swim at beaches patrolled by lifesavers (www .lifesaving.org.nz), who last year pulled over 800 people from the water.

MEDICAL SERVICES
Health care in NZ is of a high standard and inexpensive by international standards. While NZ doesn't have a government-funded system of public hospitals, all travellers are covered for medical care resulting from accidents that occur in the country. Costs incurred for the treatment of medical illnesses can generally be recouped through travel insurance – providing you have coverage!

Hospitals with 24-hour accident and emergency departments:

Ascot Accident & Medical Clinic (3, B3; ☎ 520 9555; 90 Greenlane Rd East, Remuera)

Auckland City Hospital (4, C5; ☎ 379 7440; Park Rd, Grafton)

DENTAL SERVICES
Should you chip a tooth or require emergency treatment, head to **Auckland Emergency Dental Service** (3, A3; ☎ 630 4796; 520 Mt Eden Rd, Mt Eden).

PHARMACIES
The **Urgent Pharmacy** (4, E6; ☎ 520 6634; 60 Broadway, Newmarket) is open til 1am.

Holidays
New Year 1 & 2 January
Auckland Anniversary 29 January
Waitangi Day 6 February
Easter: Good Friday & Easter Monday March/April
Anzac Day 25 April
Queen's Birthday First Monday in June
Labour Day Fourth Monday in October
Christmas Day 25 December
Boxing Day 26 December

Internet
INTERNET SERVICE PROVIDERS
The country's main telecommunications company is **Telecom** (www.telecom.co.nz), with around 200 wireless hot spots around the city. If you have a wi-fi-enabled device, you can purchase a Telecom wireless prepaid card from participating wireless hotspot venues, or get a prepaid number (from the log-in page at any wireless hot spot, you can purchase an online number using a credit card). The cost is $10 per hour.

Local Internet Service Providers (ISPs):
Clear.Net (☎ 0508 888 800; www.clear .net.nz)
Earthlight (☎ 03-479 0303; www .earthlight.co.nz) Has a page on its website detailing prepaid Internet access for travellers to NZ.
Telecom Xtra (☎ 0800 289 987; http:// xtra.co.nz/products)

INTERNET CAFES
Access at public libraries costs $2 per hour. Many hotels and hostels are wi-fi enabled or have a computer or two for public use. Walk any city block and you'll stumble upon an Internet café or foodmart offering access; costs are between $2 and $4 an hour. You might try **Discount Dialling** (2, B2; ☎ 355 7300; 7 Fort St, Auckland) or **I-Life Zone** (2, B3; ☎ 309 2533; 327 Queen St, Auckland).

USEFUL WEBSITES
Lonely Planet's website (www.lonelyplanet .com) has links to many of Auckland's websites. Others to try:
Auckland Regional Council (www.arc .govt.nz) Parks information.
Auckland Tourism (www.aucklandnz .com)
Dine Out (www.dineout.co.nz) Locals' reviews of local eateries.
Heart of the City (www.hotcity.co.nz) Events and attractions info.
Maori (www.maori.org.nz) Stories, language and customs.

Lost Property

For items lost on a train, call ☎ 0800 467 536 368, on a bus call ☎ 442 0555 and on a ferry ☎ 367 9111. It pays to make photocopies of your important documents, keep some with you (separate from the originals) and leave a copy at home.

Metric System

NZ uses the metric system.

TEMPERATURE

$°C = (°F - 32) ÷ 1.8$
$°F = (°C \times 1.8) + 32$

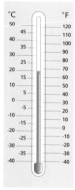

DISTANCE
1in = 2.54cm
1cm = 0.39in
1m = 3.3ft = 1.1yd
1ft = 0.3m
1km = 0.62 miles
1 mile = 1.6km

WEIGHT
1kg = 2.2lb
1lb = 0.45kg
1g = 0.04oz
1oz = 28g

VOLUME
1L = 0.26 US gallons
1 US gallon = 3.8L
1L = 0.22 imperial gallons
1 imperial gallon = 4.55L

Money
CURRENCY

The NZ dollar is made up of 100 cents: there are 10c, 20c and 50c, $1 and $2 coins, and $5, $10, $20, $50 and $100 notes. In July 2006 a new design for smaller, lighter silver coins (10c, 20c and 50c) was introduced, and the poor wee 5c coin was withdrawn from circulation, being deemed as having little value. Prices are often still marked in single cents and then rounded to the nearest 10c when you come to pay.

TRAVELLERS CHEQUES

The ubiquity of debit- and credit-card access in Auckland tends to make travellers cheques seem rather clumsy. Nevertheless, Amex, Thomas Cook and other well-known international brands of travellers cheques are easily exchanged. You need to present your passport for identification when cashing them. Fees per transaction for changing foreign-currency travellers cheques vary from bank to bank, while Amex or Travelex perform the task commission-free if you use their cheques.

CREDIT CARDS

The best way to carry most of your money is within the electronic imprint of a plastic card. Major credit cards such as Visa and MasterCard are widely accepted for everything from a hostel bed or a restaurant meal to a bungy jump or a taxi. They can also be used to get cash advances over the counter at banks and from ATMs, depending on the card. To report your card as lost, call:

American Express (☎ 336 393 1111)
MasterCard (☎ 0800 449 140)
Visa (☎ 0508 600 300)

ATMS

Twenty-four hour ATMs accompany most of Auckland's numerous bank branches. Major banks, including the Bank of New Zealand, ANZ and Westpac also accept debit cards that are linked to the international network systems (Cirrus, Maestro, Barclays Connect, etc). Shops and retail outlets use Eftpos for on-the-spot debit-card payments.

CHANGING MONEY

Foreign-exchange branches may offer marginally better exchange rates than the banks, and usually have longer opening hours and queue-free service. Most licensed moneychangers are open retail hours, with a number located downtown, especially along Queen St.

Newspapers & Magazines

Auckland's major broadsheet is the *NZ Herald* (www.nzherald.co.nz), with nationals the *Sunday Star Times* and *Sunday News* available on weekends. *Metro* magazine is the city's revered (and rightly so) current affairs magazine, which includes comment and reviews.

Opening Hours

Banks, businesses and stores are closed on public holidays. Museums and other attractions often close on Christmas Day.
Banks (🕘 9.30am-4.30pm Mon-Fri)
Post Offices (🕘 8.30am-5pm Mon-Fri) Main branches also open 9.30am to 1pm Saturday.
Restaurants (🕘 noon to 3pm & 6 to 10pm)
Shops (🕘 9am-5.30pm Mon-Wed, 9am-9pm Thu-Fri, 10am-4pm Sat & Sun)

Post

The services offered by **New Zealand Post** (☎ 0800 736 353; www.nzpost.co.nz) are reliable and reasonably inexpensive. Downtown's **main post office** (2, A3; ☎ 379 6710; Wellesley St; 🕘 7.30am-5pm Mon-Fri) is one of four dotted around town. Buy stamps from any post office and most newsagents.

POSTAL RATES

Within NZ, postage costs 45c for standard letters and postcards. Sending a letter, aerogramme or postcard anywhere in Australia and the South Pacific costs $1.50. Sending a postcard or aerogramme elsewhere in the world costs $1.50 and a letter $2.

Radio

Tune in to National Radio (101.4FM) for current affairs, and Concert FM (92.6) for classical and jazz, or one of the many commercial stations crowding the airwaves. Kiwi FM (www.kiwifm.co.nz; 102.2FM) plays only NZ music.

Telephone

Auckland's numerous public payphones are either coin- or card-operated; local calls cost 50c.

PHONECARDS

Available at newsagencies and post offices for a fixed dollar value (usually $5, $10, $20 and $50), to be used with any public or private phone by dialling a toll-free access number and then the PIN number on the card.

MOBILE PHONES

Local mobile phone numbers are preceded by the prefix ☎ 021, ☎ 025 or ☎ 027.

If you want to bring your own phone and go on a prepaid service using a local SIM card, Vodafone (www.vodafone.co.nz) will set you up with a SIM card and phone number (about $35, including $10 worth of calls), and top-ups can be purchased at newsagencies and post offices.

COUNTRY & CITY CODES

If dialling NZ from overseas:
New Zealand (☎ 64)
Auckland (☎ 9) Dial ☎ 09 if calling from elsewhere within New Zealand.

The 0800 and 0508 numbers listed in this book can only be dialled within NZ.

USEFUL PHONE NUMBERS
International Direct Dial Code (☎ 00)
International Directory Inquiries (☎ 0172)
Local Directory Inquiries (☎ 018)
Operator (☎ 0)
Weather (☎ 0900 999 09)

Television

There are six free-to-air commercial TV stations: TV One (news, current affairs and entertainment), TV2 (soaps, movies and music), TV3 and C4, Prime, and Maori TV, plus the subscriber service Sky TV.

Time

Auckland Standard Time is 12 hours ahead of GMT/UTC. Daylight savings time is practised from the first Sunday in October to the third Sunday of the following March.

Tipping

Tipping is optional in Auckland; however, a gratuity of between 5% and 10% of restaurant bills and cab fares is the norm.

Tourist Information

Auckland Visitor Information Centre (2, A3; ☎ 363 7182; www.aucklandnz .com; cnr Victoria & Federal Sts; ☺ 8am-8pm) In the Sky Tower Atrium.

Department of Conservation Information Centre (DOC; 2, B1; ☎ 379 6476; www.doc.govt.nz; Ferry Bldg, 99 Quay St; ☺ 10am-5.30pm Mon-Fri, to 3pm Sat)

Discover New Zealand Centre (2, B1; ☎ 307 4000; www.discovernewzealand .com; 180 Quay St; ☺ 9am-5pm)

Domestic Airport Visitors Centre (3, B6; ☎ 256 8480; ☺ 7am-5pm) In the Air New Zealand section of the domestic airport.

NZ Visitors Centre (2, B1; ☎ 307 0612; 137 Quay St; ☺ 8.30am-6pm Mon-Fri, 9am-5pm Sat & Sun) At Princes Wharf, covers the entire country.

Visitors Information Centre (3, B6; ☎ 275 6467; international airport; ☺ 1st flight-last flight) Left of the customs-hall exit.

LANGUAGE

English and Maori are NZ's official languages. While English dominates, one in three Aucklanders are either Maori, Pacific Islander or Asian.

Index

See also separate subindexes for Eating (p61), Entertainment (p61), Shopping (p61), Sights with map references (p62) and Sleeping (p62).

FEATURES

Antoines	*Eating*
Silo Theatre	*Entertainment*
Minus 5° Bar	*Drinking*
Sky Tower	*Highlights*
Pauanesia	*Shopping*
Ewelme Cottage	*Sights/Activities*
Fringe of Heaven	*Sleeping*
Waiheke Island	*Trips & Tours*

AREAS

	Airport
	Beach, Desert
	Building
	Land
	Mall
	Other Area
	Park/Cemetery
	Sports
	Urban

HYDROGRAPHY

	River, Creek
	Intermittent River
	Canal
	Mudflats
	Water

BOUNDARIES

	State, Provincial
	Regional, Suburb

ROUTES

	Tollway
	Freeway
	Primary Road
	Secondary Road
	Tertiary Road
	Lane
	Under Construction
	One-Way Street
	Unsealed Road
	Mall/Steps
	Tunnel
	Walking Path
	Walking Trail/Track
	Pedestrian Overpass
	Walking Tour

TRANSPORT

	Airport, Airfield
	Bus Route
	Cycling, Bicycle Path
	Ferry
	General Transport
	Metro
	Monorail
	Rail
	Taxi Rank
	Tram

SYMBOLS

	Bank, ATM
	Beach
	Castle, Fortress
	Christian
	Diving, Snorkelling
	Embassy, Consulate
	Hospital, Clinic
	Information
	Internet Access
	Lighthouse
	Lookout
	Monument
	Mountain, Volcano
	National Park
	Parking Area
	Petrol Station
	Picnic Area
	Point of Interest
	Police Station
	Post Office
	Swimming Pool
	Ruin
	Telephone
	Toilets
	Waterfall
	Winery, Vineyard
	Zoo, Bird Sanctuary

24/7 travel advice
www.lonelyplanet.com